ISAIAH 53

ISAIAH 53

COMPILED BY
STANLEY BARNES

AMBASSADOR

Belfast Northern Ireland **Greenville** South Carolina

Isaiah 53
© Copyright 2000 Stanley Barnes

ISBN 1 84030 078 7

Ambassador Publications
a division of
Ambassador Productions Ltd.
Providence House
Ardenlee Street,
Belfast,
BT6 8QJ
Northern Ireland
www.ambassador-productions.com

Emerald House
427 Wade Hampton Blvd.
Greenville
SC 29609, USA
www.emeraldhouse.com

Introduction

ISAIAH 53 IS ONE OF THE MOST WONDERFUL AND PRECIOUS CHAPTERS IN THE ENTIRE BIBLE.

Martin Luther, the great reformer, said that 'it ought to be written on parchment of gold and lettered in diamonds.'

Thomas Manton the puritan, stated, 'Isaiah 53 may rather be called the Gospel than the prophecy of Isaiah. It contains so ample and clear a discovery of Jesus Christ, that one would rather account it historical than prophetical. Other prophecies are explained by the history of Christ in the New Testament, but this prophecy explains the history.'

The central theme of this great prophecy is Christ's substitutionary work on the cross on behalf of His people. Here are eleven sermons which are among the best to be found on the subject. Famous pulpiteers such as Moody, Spurgeon, Meyer and others, provide masterful interpretations and Gospel applications of the 'holy of holies' of Isaiah's presentation of the Suffering Servant.

STANLEY BARNES

Contents

❦ Frederick Brotherton Meyer

Frederick Brotherton Meyer was born in London, England on the 8th April, 1847. He was the son of a wealthy family of German descent and was converted to Christ as a young child of five years. After graduating from London University he completed his theological training at Regents Park Baptist College and while he was a student he ministered for a year at Duke Street Baptist Chapel, Richmond, Surrey. In 1872 he became the pastor of Priory Street Baptist Chapel in York, where he met D. L. Moody. He courageously opened his church to Moody and Sankey despite much opposition. During the course of his ministry he successfully pastored several churches, and became a popular speaker at many well known conventions including Keswick where he became a firm favourite. He was a prolific writer of some seventy books, including ten books on great men of the Old Testament and three on those of the New Testament. This sermon is taken from his exposition Christ In Isaiah.

Chapter One

FAITH AS A SWITCH

'If thou couldest trust, poor soul,
In Him who rules the whole,
Thou wouldst find peace and rest,
Wisdom and sight are well; but Trust is best.'
                                        - A. Procter

'WHO HATH BELIEVED OUR REPORT? AND TO WHOM IS THE ARM OF THE LORD
REVEALED?' — ISAIAH 53:1

'JESUS SAITH UNTO HER, SAID I NOT UNTO THEE, THAT, IF THOU WOULDEST
BELIEVE, THOU SHOULDEST SEE THE GLORY OF GOD?' — JOHN 11:40

A LAWYER WHOM I KNOW TOOK ME THE OTHER DAY TO SEE THE
FIRE-PROOF STRONG ROOM IN WHICH HE KEEPS VALUABLE DEEDS
and securities. It is excavated under the street, and a passage leads far
into the interior, lined on either side with receptacles for the precious
documents. On entering, he took up what appeared to be a candle, with

a cord attached to it; the other end he deftly fastened to a switch at the entrance, by means of which the electricity which was waiting there poured up the wire hidden in the cord, glowed at the wick of the china-candle, and we were able to pass to the end of the passage, uncoiling cord and wire as we went. That unlighted candle resembles the Christian worker, apart from the power of the Holy Ghost. Faith may be compared to the switch by means of which the saving might of God pours into our life and ministry.

It cannot be too strongly insisted on, that our faith is the absolute condition and measure of the exertion of God's saving might. No faith, no blessing; little faith, little blessing; great faith, great blessing. According to our faith, so it is always done to us. The saving might of God's glorious arm may be waiting close against us; but it is inoperative unless we are united to it by faith.

The negative and positive sides of this great and important truth are presented in the texts before us; one of which complains that the arm of God is not revealed, because men have not believed the inspired report; the other affirms from the lips of the Master, that those who believe shall see the glory of God. The texts between them will help us to understand why some, who are best equipped for service, fail; while others, with very indifferent equipment, achieve great and lasting success.

I. THE ARM OF GOD

This expression is often used in the older Scriptures, and everywhere signifies the active, saving energy of the Most High. We first meet with it in his own address to Moses: 'I will redeem them with a stretched-out arm.' Then, in the triumphant shout that broke from two million glad voices beside the Red Sea – and frequently in the book of Deuteronomy, - we read of the stretched-out arm of Jehovah. It is a favourite phrase with the poets and prophets of Israel – the arm that redeems; the holy arm; the glorious arm; the bared arm of God. We have already noticed how it is bidden awake, and put on strength. This metaphor is somewhat different.

The conception is that, owing to the unbelief of Israel, it lies inoperative, hidden under the heavy folds of Oriental drapery; whereas it might be revealed, raising itself aloft in vigorous and effective effort.

ALL THAT CONCERNS US NOW IS THE RELATION BETWEEN FAITH AND THE FORTH-PUTTING OF GOD'S SAVING MIGHT. God's arm was revealed at the Red Sea, making a path through its depths by which his ransomed might pass over. Then Moses' faith was in eager and triumphant exercise, and the people believed the report which he had given of the words of Jehovah. But it sank into repose during the long forty years of wandering, because Israel believed not his word.

God's arm was revealed at the Jordan, and through the remarkable career of Joshua; it cleft the river at flood, overthrew the walls of Jericho, chased in flight the armies of the aliens, restrained the deepening shadows of the night, and gave the Land of Promise to the chosen race; and this, because Joshua never wavered in his strong, heroic confidence. But again it sank paralysed and powerless to rest, when, in the days of the judges, the people ceased to exercise the faith to which nothing was impossible. Whenever the fire gleamed up from the dull, white ash, as in the days of Gideon, Barak, Jephthah, and Samson, instantly the arm of the Lord was made bare.

The arm of the Lord was revealed in the days when David's faith realised that the living Lord was still amongst his people, well able to save without mail, or spear, or shield. What a springtide was that! The birds of holy song warbled sweetly under a clear heaven of love; the flowerets of nobility, righteousness, and truth begemmed the soil: the light was that of a morning without clouds. There was no standing against the onset of the soldiers, who in the cave of Adullam had acquired lessons of heroic faith as well as those of knightly chivalry. But again the arm of God relapsed into quiescence, and allowed the foes of his people to work their will even to their captivity, because Israel's faith had become like the Temple of Solomon, a desecrated and ruined shrine.

As we are taught in the Epistle to the Hebrews, all the great exploits and episodes of Hebrew story were due to the faith which believed that God is a present force in history, and a Rewarder of those who diligently seek Him.

2. THE LIFE OF THE SON OF MAN.

As this chapter suggests, it seemed, from many points of view, a failure. The arm of the Lord was in Him, though hidden from all save the handful who believed. Probably our Lord never wrought a miracle, unless faith was in exercise on the part either of the recipients or spectators of his saving help. The centurion, though a Gentile; the Syrophoenician woman, though accounted a dog; the leper, though an outcast pariah – drew from Him virtue that healed and saved: whilst the bulk of the nation, and especially the companions of his early life, missed the benediction, which had come so nigh them, because they enwrapt themselves in proud indifference. Through unbelief the branches were deprived of the richness of the Root of David. And the condition of Israel in the world today is due to persistent unbelief, which has cut them off from the help of the right arm of the Lord.

3. A SPECIMEN CASE.

For two days Christ had lingered beyond the Jordan, though urgently needed in Bethany, where life was ebbing fast, and tears were flowing which were not wholly due to the sickness and death of him whom Jesus loved. A sense of forlornness; an inability to account for the delayed advent of the dearest Friend, who neither came nor sent word – made those tears more bitter. The Master, however, was keenly sensitive to all that was taking place. He knew that sickness had become death, and said presently, 'Our friend Lazarus sleepeth.' That interval of silence and absence seems to have been filled with prayer; to which He referred in the words He spoke aloud at the grave, that the people might be led to attribute all the glory to his Father, and to appreciate the love and beauty of his character. Before our Lord left his hiding-place He knew that the Father had granted Him, in his human nature, the life of his friend. 'I go,' said he, 'to awake him out of sleep. I was glad that I was not there to stay the fall of life's ebbing tide; because, in raising him from the dead, such a proof will be furnished of my oneness with Jehovah, as to compel your faith, and be a comfort and inspiration in all after days.'

But even though our Lord went to Bethany with the assurance that the arm of the Lord would certainly be made bare, yet he must of necessity have the co-operation and sympathy of some one's faith.

SUCH FAITH HE DISCOVERED IN MARTHA. This is startling, and helpful. We should not have been surprised to learn that it was found in Mary; because her still and spiritual nature was so closely akin to his own – she had drunk so deeply into his words; she was capable of such a white-heat of love, consecration, and self-forgetting devotion. But we should not have expected Martha to manifest faith, to connect the stored life of Jesus with the charnel-house where Lazarus lay, four days dead. Yet so it befell. She met Jesus with the assurance that He possessed power enough to have averted death, had He only been in time; she declared her belief that his prayer could secure its will from God, and confessed that for long, in her secret soul, she had believed that Jesus was the Messiah, the Son of God, the long-expected Redeemer. These admissions on her part showed that faith was already within her soul, as a grain of mustard-seed, awaiting the summertide of God's presence, the education of his grace.

There are many earnest Christians, whose energies are taxed to the utmost by their ministry to others. Philanthropists, housewives, workers in every department of Christian service – such are their engagements that they have no time to sit quietly at the feet of Christ, or mature great schemes of loving sympathy with his plans, as Mary did when she prepared her anointing-oil for her Lord's burial. And yet they are capable of a great faith. Beneath the bustle and rush of life, the impulses of the Divine are being responded to; faith in the living Saviour is ripening to a golden harvest; forces are being generated which will surprise themselves and others. Christ will one day discover, reveal, and educate that faith to great exploits.

HE PUT A PROMISE BEFORE HER. 'Thy brother shall rise again.' Faith feeds on promises, as the spark that trembles on the hearth grows by the fuel heaped on and around it. If we consider circumstances, we stagger and faint. But if we look away to the strong clear words of God, and through them to the Promiser, we become, like Abraham, strong in faith, and sure that what God has promised He is able also to perform. Make much of God's Word: faith cometh by hearing. Listen to the report – it will induce belief, and this will secure the revelation of the Almighty arm.

HE SHOWED THAT ITS FULFILMENT MIGHT BE EXPECTED HERE AND NOW. Martha was quite prepared to believe that Lazarus would rise again at the last day; but she had no faith in the immediate vivification of the body that lay in its niche behind the stone. Jesus said, 'I AM the Resurrection and the Life. Here and now is the power which, on that day of which you speak, shall awaken the dead; do but believe, and you shall see that resurrection anticipated.'

Ponder the force of this I AM. It is the present tense of the Eternal. At the burning bush, it was the first lesson that Moses had to learn. God is the I AM. He is; He is here; He is able and willing to do now all that He ever will do in the days that are yet to be. Man is so apt to postpone the miraculous and Divine, till some dim horizon-line has been attained and passed. God has blessed, and He will bless. God did marvels at the first Advent, and He will repeat them at the second. But the present is the period of Divine absenteeism – so we think. Oh to believe that Jesus is waiting to be all that He has ever been to souls, or will be! Oh to hear Him say, 'I am Resurrection to the dead: I am the more abundant Life to all who live and believe in Me'!

HE AROUSED HER EXPECTANCY. For what other reason did He ask that the stone might be rolled away? It is certain that it would have been perfectly easy for his voice to reach the ear of the dead through the stony doorway; and had He willed it, Lazarus could have emerged from the grave, though the stone still sealed its mouth. Almost certainly the direction to remove the stone was intended to awaken Martha's expectation and hope that the arm of the Lord would presently be revealed. And it had the desired result. With quickened eagerness she endeavoured to arrest obedience to his mandate; and when the Lord persisted, and reminded her that this

was the opportunity for her faith, her soul leaped up to receive with
ardour the blessing He was there to give. She believed, and she beheld
the glory of God in the face of Jesus Christ.

The one aim for each of us should be to bring Christ and the dead
Lazarus together. Death can no more exist when He is present, than night
when the sun is rising. Corruption, impurity, sin, flee before Him to whom
the Father gave to have life in Himself, and who came that we might have
life, and have it more abundantly. Let your faith make an inlet for the
Life-giver into your circle of society, your church, your class, your home.
Nothing will suffice if this is lacking. Eloquence, learning, position, these
will fail. But faith, though it be of the weakest, simplest nature, will link
the Saviour, who is alive for evermore, and has the keys of death
and Hades, with those who have been in the graves of sin so long that
corruption has asserted its foul dominion over every part of their nature.

Let us ask Christ, our Saviour, to work such faith in us; to develop it
by every method of education and discipline; to mature it by his nurturing
Spirit, until the arm of God is revealed in us and through us, and the
glory of God is manifested before the gaze of men.

At the same time, it is not well to concentrate our thought too
much on FAITH, lest we hinder its growth. Look away from faith to the
object of faith will spring of itself. It is the bloom of the soul's health. See
to it that thy soul is nourished and at rest: then faith will be as natural as
scent to a flower, or bloom to a peach. Do not ask if thy faith is of the
right sort; all faith is right, which is directed towards Him, whom God
hath set forth to receive the loving devotion of all human hearts.

❦ JOHN DANIEL JONES

John Daniel Jones was born in Ruthin, Wales in 1865. After his ordination in 1889, he became the pastor of Newland Church in Lincoln, Wales. Following this, he accepted the call to be the pastor of Richmond Hill Congregational Church in Bournemouth, England, where he ministered for thirty-nine years, retiring in 1937. He published many books of sermons including THE HOPE OF THE GOSPEL, from which this sermon, A ROOT OUT OF DRY GROUND is taken.

His other books include, THE GOSPEL OF THE SOVEREIGNTY AND OTHER SERMONS, THE LORD OF LIFE AND DEATH (sermons based on John 11), THE WAY INTO THE KINGDOM (on the beattitudes) and THE KING OF LOVE (meditations on the 23rd Psalm).

He died on Sunday, 19th April 1942, and the inscription on his gravestone in Bournemouth Cemetery reads, "John Daniel Jones, Preacher of the Gospel. 'Simply To Thy Cross I Cling.'"

Chapter two

A ROOT OUT OF DRY GROUND

'FOR HE SHALL GROW UP BEFORE HIM AS A TENDER PLANT, AND AS A ROOT OUT
OF A DRY GROUND...' - ISAIAH 53:2

'A ROOT OUT OF A DRY GROUND'! WHAT IDEA DOES THIS
FIGURE SUGGEST TO YOU? IT SUGGESTS TO ME THE IDEA OF
unexpectedness, unaccountableness, miraculousness. A 'dry ground' -
that is not exactly the kind of place we expect a root to shoot from. A 'dry
ground' - that is not exactly the kind of soil in which we expect plants to
flourish. I notice that when the bedding-out season comes round,
gardeners, even when they put their plants into prepared ground, take
care to keep that ground moistened and well watered. If they bedded
their plants in dry ground, they would not spring up at all. If a man took
it into his head to plant seeds on our highways, he need not look for
flowers in the spring. They are dry ground. And if by chance a root should
spring up out of a dry ground, it is usually a very poor and stunted and
shrivelled thing. Some time ago as I travelled through one of the Welsh
mining valleys my eye fell upon three or four trees that were growing out
of the midst of a hill of coal waste. It was a most unlikely place in which

to see a tree growing at all, and I marvelled at the vitality that could exist amid such surroundings. But I also noticed that it was a very precarious and poverty-stricken existence these trees on the coal heap were leading. Compared with the trees that were growing in the green and fertile fields near by, they were poor and sickly-looking specimens. It is hopeless to expect a strong, vigorous, beautiful plant to spring out of a dry ground.

But the prophet here asserts that, in the case of a certain historic Person, that hopeless and seemingly impossible thing actually happened. 'He grew up before him,' he writes, 'as a root out of a dry ground.' I need scarcely say to remind you that the Messiah is the subject of this great and overwhelming chapter. It may be, as scholars assert, that it was the afflicted nation of Israel that the prophet at first pictured under the figure of the suffering servant. But in this chapter 53, he has come to identify God's suffering Servant, not with the whole nation, but with one particular Person in it. In a word, in this moving chapter the prophet, by the Spirit, speaks of Christ. And this is one feature about the Christ which he notices - His unexpectedness, His unaccountableness, His miraculousness. He grew up before Him as a 'root out of a dry ground.' There was nothing in the soil out of which He grew to account for Jesus. The marvel of Christ's Person becomes all the more marvellous when we consider the conditions of His time and the circumstances out of which He sprang. The nature of the growth is always in accordance with the nature of the soil. You cannot expect a harvest from seed that falls on the rocky ground. If things grow at all out of dry and hard ground, they are bound to be feeble and sickly growths. But Jesus was no feeble and sickly growth. He was the 'chiefest among ten thousand, and the altogether lovely.' He was like the cedar of Lebanon for strength, like the lily of the valley for fragrance and purity, like the rose of Sharon for glory. By universal consent He was the best and noblest, and the highest and holiest of mankind, and yet He grew up as a root out of a dry ground. There was nothing in His circumstances or surroundings to account for Him or explain Him. He is as surprising, as inexplicable, as miraculous as would be, let us say, a crop of flowers springing up out of the asphalt paving of our public streets.

This, then, is the subject upon which I want to speak - the unexpectedness of Jesus. If you rule out all but humanitarian considerations, He remains as inexplicable as a 'root springing up out of a dry ground.'

FAMILY

First of all, there is nothing in His family to account for Him. We make much in these days of the influence of heredity. Sometimes I begin to feel we make too much - that we press the doctrine of heredity so far that we endanger individuality and personal responsibility. But while I think that sometimes we are inclined to press the effects of heredity too far, that it does play a large part in human development is beyond cavil or dispute. Heredity is one of the factors that go to determine character and destiny. Parents reproduce themselves in their children. We inherit from our parents not only facial and physical characteristics, we inherit from them also mental gifts and moral qualities. Life supplies us with abundant illustrations of all this. We speak in England here sometimes of our 'ruling families.' Sometimes we do so angrily and resentfully. We are inclined to think and to say that certain families monopolize the government simply in virtue of their rank and birth. But really that is not so. Rank will not keep a man long in the ruler's place if the man himself is a fool. If we have ruling families it is because there is in such families a certain capactiy for rule. Take the Cecils. Possibly we do not always agree with them. But no-one can think of the Cecil family, from the great Elizabethan statesman downwards, without seeing that they possess a certain hereditary gift and aptitude for government. Government has become a tradition with them, and succeeding generations display an amazing instinct and aptitude for rule. And it is the recognition that gifts and qualities often descend from father to son, from parent to child, that makes biographers of great men begin their story with some account of the ancestry from whom their particular hero is descended. They do so because oftentimes acquaintance with a great man's parentage and remoter ancestry will help us to explain the great man himself.

But the study of Christ's ancestry does not help us in the least little bit to explain Christ. There is nothing in His family to account for Him. We know this on the testimony, not of Christ's friends, but on the testimony of His critics and foes. You remember Mark's account of our Lord's visit to Nazareth? The effect of His preaching was to create a feeling of wonderment and amazement among His hearers. 'Many hearing him,' says Mark, 'were astonished, saying, From whence hath this man these things? and what wisdom is this which is given unto him, that even such mighty works are wrought by his hands?' The wonder would have been great had Jesus been the son of some great and learned rabbi. It was absolutely staggering when they thought of the house from which He had actually issued. 'Is not this,' they said in bewildered astonishment, 'the son of Mary, the brother of James, and Joses, and Judas and Simon? and are not these his sisters here with us?' They knew all about Christ's family. It was not His likeness to them that struck them, but His total unlikeness. When they remembered that Mary was His mother, and James, and Joses and Judas and Simon His brothers, they wondered how Jesus could have come out of such a family circle. For Mary was just a plain peasant woman. And James and Joses and Judas and Simon were quite ordinary and humdrum men. You can see James for yourself in the epistle that bears his name. The man that reveals himself in that epistle - and from his position in the Jerusalem church we are justified in arguing that he was the ablest of the brothers - is a dry, bald, rather narrow man, with a good fund of common sense, but without any glint of the soaring vision that distinguished the Lord. There is all the difference between James and Jesus there is between a half penny dip and the noonday sun. Even the prejudiced Jews felt and acknowledged this difference; they looked at James - good, plain, commonplace man; then they listened to Jesus speaking His wonderful words of spirit and life, and, I repeat, they were left in a condition of bewildered amazement. 'What is the wisdom that is given to this man?' they asked. There was nothing in our Lord's heredity to account for Him. As far as His family was concerned, He grew up as a root 'out of a dry ground.'

SURROUNDINGS

Then, in the second place, there was nothing in His surroundings to account for Him. Next to heredity, we moderns are inclined to lay chief stress upon environment. A man is largely made, we say, by the conditions under which he is constrained to spend his life - by the moral and intellectual atmosphere he breathes, by the company he keeps, by the education he receives, and so on. Now this truth, again, is often pressed to extremes. From the way in which some people state it, you might believe that everyone bred in a pious home grows up pious, and everyone reared in a slum grows up slummy both in body and mind. But life and experience prove that this is not so. Environment is not a determining factor; in the last resort man can always rise superior to it. But while it does not exercise decisive and determining influence, it remains true that it does exert a large and important influence. A man's environment always colours his mode of speech, his manners, his whole mental and intellectual outlook. For instance, here we are living in the twentieth century. The twentieth century puts its unmistakable mark upon us: we speak its language; we use its measure of knowledge; we think its thoughts and beliefs. If any of us are guilty of making books, and so adding to that much study which the wise man declares is a weariness to the flesh, there is no need to put a date of publication on the front page. An examination of the contents will always be sufficient to locate the book within, at any rate, a few years of its right date. For involuntarily we reproduce in our books the ideas current in our day. They proclaim themselves as belonging to the beginning of the twentieth century. In the matter of thought and intellectual outlook we are the children of our time.

Or take, again, the matter of culture. The kind of culture we have received always leaves its mark. Let us suppose man has received no education worth speaking of. The lack will reveal itself in his speech, and not simply in his speech, but in his manners and tastes and whole intellectual outlook. On the other hand, if a man has enjoyed the advantage of a university training, that will also reveal itself, not simply in the correctness of his speech, but in something far more important, a certain unmistakable breadth of mind. The peasant lives in his narrow, contracted peasant world; the scholar lives in the vast and glorious universe which scholarship opens to him. Environment exercises enormous influence. I will not say a man is entirely made, but he is largely made by his surroundings.

But surroundings entirely fail to account for Jesus. He came from a humble peasant home. His reputed father was a carpenter in a Galilean village. The household - it is obvious from scattered hints in the Gospel - was a poor household. Joseph and Mary did not, as some poor Scottish parents do, scrape and sacrifice in order to send their son to a university. They were probably too poor to dream of sending their boy to Jerusalem to sit with Saul at the feet of Gamaliel. All they could do in the way of education was to give him such as the village school at Nazareth provided. And even that education was not prolonged. The family expenses grew as one little child after another made its advent, and Jesus was taken from school and put to help His father in the workshop, and for fourteen or fifteen years He shared in Joseph's trade - He was one of the village joiners. And yet this Jesus, Himself a working man, bred in a working home and blessed with nothing beyond a peasant boy's education, 'spake as never yet man spake.' He surpassed in wisdom the greatest, wisest, holiest men of His own great, holy, and inspired race. There is nothing in His surroundings to account for it.

You cannot explain it on the ground of early advantages, for He had none. I do not wonder that the Jews were surprised. 'Whence hath this Man these things?' they asked. 'Is not this the carpenter?' 'How knoweth this Man letters,' they asked on another occasion, 'having never learned?' They thought of our Lord's home, they thought of His education, they thought of Nazareth, they thought of those years in the workshop; and then they thought of His words of grace, His deeds of power, and His life of absolute holiness, and it left them utterly and hopelessly bewildered. There was nothing in His upbringing and surroundings to account for Him. As far as His environment was concerned, He grew up as a 'root out of a dry ground.'

TIME

Then, in the third place, as there was nothing in His own immediate surroundings at Nazareth, so was there nothing in the mental and moral atmosphere of His time to account for Jesus. Now, there appear to occur in history certain seasons or cycles that seem to favour the emergence of genius. For instance, 'the spacious days of Queen Elizabeth,' in our own country, witnessed a wonderful efflorescence of gift and genius in almost every department of human endeavour. The new learning had but just reached England, and it created a new and vigorous life, with the result that England had great men in her councils, great sailors on her seas, and a great galaxy of poets to adorn her literature. But the days in which Jesus appeared were not such spacious days. Never did the national life of the Jew run so poor and thin. The chief glory of the Jew was his religion. But all the days from Malachi to Jesus were poor days for religion. You might say of them as the Bible says of those disastrous days of Eli - 'There was no open vision.' The oracles were dumb. There was no authentic divine voice. Religion had degenerated into legalism, and legalism issued in hypocrisy. The prophets had all died out, and the scribes, with their dry and thin pedantries, took their place. There was nothing in the condition of Israel favourable to the emergence of a great religious genius. There was no religious expectancy, no spiritual life. I think of Judea in these first years of the Christian era, and then I think of Jesus. The contemplation of the one does not help me to understand the other. As far as the religious condition of His day is concerned, Jesus is a 'root out of a dry ground.'

And not only is there nothing in the religious condition of our Lord's time to account for His appearance, but there is nothing in the state of religious thought to account for His teaching. I said a moment ago that we are all of us, in a very deep and unmistakable sense, the children of our time. In our ideas and beliefs we reproduce the ideas and beliefs current in our own day. But Jesus is in no sense a child of His day. That is not to say that, in historical and scientific matters, He did not share the current beliefs of His time. But Jesus' sphere was neither history nor science, but religion. He did not come to anticipate Galileo and Newton and Darwin. He came to show men the Father. And in the matter of religion Jesus was in no sense a child of His own day. The comment of the people who heard Him preach was that He was 'not as their scribes.' The rabbi who came to Him by night was so staggered by His teaching about the kingdom that he cried, 'How can these things be?' The charge brought against the first disciples was that by their teaching they were turning the world upside down. It was not the familiarity of our Lord's religious ideas, but their strangeness, their absolute newness, their revolutionizing character, that astonished His contemporaries. The fatherhood of God was not a religious idea of His time. The spirituality of worship was not a religious idea of His time. The new birth was not a religious idea of His time. The supremacy of love was not a religious idea of His time. The universality of the kingdom was not a religious idea of His time. I think of the Jews of our Lord's day identifying ritual with religion, dreaming of a material empire, and thinking that the kingdom was a Jewish preserve; and then I think of Jesus revealing the Father, declaring that God was a Spirit, and must be worshipped in spirit and in truth; preaching a spiritual kingdom, into which publicans and sinners, Greeks and Gentiles reborn, were free to enter, and into which no Jew could hope to enter until he was reborn; and I cannot find in the one any explanation of the other. On mere humanitarian grounds you cannot explain how Jesus so completely and absolutely transcended the thoughts and beliefs of His own time. You cannot understand how, such being the intellectual and spiritual atmosphere of His day, Jesus came to be able to speak these deep and eternal words of truth and life. A study of contemporary thought and faith will not enable you to account for the Sermon on the Mount or the fourteenth chapter of John. As far as the religious thought of His day is concerned, Jesus is a 'root out of a dry ground.'

RACE

And, lastly, there was nothing in our Lord's race and nationality to account for Him. I am well aware that the Jew had, shall I say, a genius for religion. I am not forgetting that from the Jewish race came forth such great and inspired seers and psalmists and prophets as Moses, and David, and the writer of this immortal prophecy from which my text is taken. But his Jewish birth and lineage do not account for Jesus. The remarkable thing about our Lord is that there is nothing exclusively Jewish about Him. Moses and David and Isaiah never allow you to forget for one moment that they are Jews. It is for Israel that they write. It is the glory of Israel they predict. It is a kingdom of Israel of which they dream. But there is nothing parochial or sectional about Jesus. He is catholic and universal. I can detect no Jewish accent in His speech. He speaks with equal directness and force to all human hearts. There is nothing foreign about Him. Like His disciples at Pentecost, He speaks to every man in the language wherein he was born. As far as the Jewish nation is concerned, Jesus is a 'root out of a dry ground.' There is nothing in His nationality to account for Him.

And I will broaden my statement and say not only that there is nothing in the Jewish nation - there is nothing even in the human race to explain Jesus. You may remind me that the race has produced great teachers and leaders like Confucius and Buddha and Mahomet and Plato and Socrates. Yes, I know; but the fact that the race produced Confucius and Buddha and Mahomet and Socrates and Plato and Dante and Shakespeare does not make it a whit easier to understand how it could produce Jesus. For in the matter of wisdom and truth, a whole universe separates Jesus from the best and wisest of other teachers. There are falsities mixed up with their wisdom, but the wisdom of Jesus is all pure gold. We outgrow their teaching. The teaching of Jesus, after nineteen centuries, remains our wonder and our inspiration. Others guess at truth. Jesus talks about the eternities in the calm and assured accents of full and perfect knowledge.

But wisdom and truth are not the most wonderful characteristics of Jesus. Holiness is the most wonderful of all. I look abroad upon the human race, and I notice wherever I look that man has a sort of taint in the blood. 'There is none that doeth good; no not one.' That terrible thing which the Bible calls sin - I see it everywhere. And the best and noblest of men are just the men who are most vividly and keenly conscious of it. The whole race, somehow, has become infected and corrupted. Original sin, and the corruption of men's hearts, are not theological doctrines, they are terrible facts of experience. But I look at Jesus and I see Him 'holy, harmless, undefiled and separate from sinners.' On the testimony of His foes, He was a man without fault. On the testimony of His own conscience - a far more wonderful testimony - He did no sin. I look at the race, stained, infected, corrupt, shut up, as the apostle put it, under sin; and then I look at the sinless and spotless Jesus. Can that stainless Person issue from that sin-stained race? Can such a stream, so fresh and sweet, issue from so bitter a fountain? If the race could produce one Jesus, why has it not produced some more? I look at the race and then at Jesus, and I can see nothing in the one to account for the other. The race could not produce Jesus. The race did not produce Jesus. Human nature is not equal to this great creation. The soil will not account for the flower. As far as the race is concerned, Jesus is a 'root out of a dry ground.'

What, then, shall we say of Jesus? There is only one thing that can be said of Him. He is not the product of race. He is the gift of God. Start from purely human considerations, and Jesus remains as big a problem and as hopeless and insoluble a riddle as a root out of a dry ground. But my difficulties vanish and I can understand Jesus when, with the holy church, I say that Jesus does not represent so much the ascent of man, as the descent of God; not so much the climbing of the human into the Divine, and the condescension of the Divine to the human; that His birth was not a mere birth, but an Incarnation; that Jesus is not simply Son of Mary, but Immanuel, God with us. 'I say,' said Browning, and I say it with him -

The acknowledgement of God in Christ,
Accepted by the reason solves for thee
All questions in the earth and out of it.

🌺 CHARLES HADDON SPURGEON

Charles Haddon Spurgeon is undoubtedly the most famous Baptist minister of the nineteenth century. Converted in 1850, he preached his first sermon at the age of sixteen.

When he was eighteen he was invited to become the pastor of the Baptist congregation at Waterbeach, Cambridgeshire. Two years later, he was called to New Park Street Church in London and within a year of his ministry the church was filled to overflowing. By the time he was twenty-two years of age he was London's most popular preacher, and in order to facilitate the vast crowds who flocked to hear him preach, a much larger building, the Metropolitan Tabernacle, was built in 1861. It seated six thousand, and until his death in 1892, was consistently filled.

During the construction of the Tabernacle, Spurgeon preached to crowds of ten thousand in the Surrey Gardens Music Hall, and on one occasion, at the youthful age of twenty-three, he preached to twenty-four thousand in the Crystal Palace.

In 1855, he bagan to publish his sermons every Thursday, at the price of one penny, and today they make up the fifty-seven volumes of THE METROPOLITAN TABERNACLE PULPIT. This sermon was delivered by Spurgeon at the Metropolitan Tabernacle, on the morning of March 2nd, 1873.

Chapter three

THE MAN OF SORROWS

'... A MAN OF SORROWS, AND ACQUAINTED WITH GRIEF...' - ISAIAH 53:3

POSSIBLY A MURMUR WILL PASS ROUND THE CONGREGATION, 'THIS IS A DREARY SUBJECT AND A MOURNFUL THEME.' BUT, O beloved, it is not so, for great as were the woes of our Redeemer, they are all over now, and are to be looked back upon with sacred triumph. However severe the struggle, the victory has been won: the labouring vessel was severely tossed by the waves, but she has now entered into the desired haven. Our Saviour is no longer in Gethsemane agonising, or upon the cross expiring; the crown of thorns has been replaced by many crowns of sovereignty; the nails and the spear have given way to the sceptre. Nor is this all, for though the suffering is ended, the blessed results never end. We may remember the travail, for the Man Child is born into the world. The sowing in tears is followed by a reaping in joy. The bruising of the heel of the woman's seed is well recompensed by the breaking of the serpent's head. It is pleasant to hear of battles fought when a decisive victory has ended war and established peace. So that the double reflection that all the work of suffering is finished by the

Redeemer, and that, henceforth, he beholds the success of all his labours, we shall rejoice, even while we enter into fellowship with his sufferings.

Let it never be forgotten that the subject of the sorrows of the Savioour has proved to be more efficacious for comfort to mourners than any other theme in the compass of revelation, or out of it. Even the glories of Christ afford no such consolation to afflicted spirits as the sufferings of Christ. Christ is in all attitudes the consolation of Israel, but he is most so as a man of sorrows. Troubled spirits turn not so much to Bethlehem as to Calvary; they prefer Gethsemane to Nazareth. The afflicted do not so much look for comfort to Christ as he will come a second time in splendour of state, as to Christ as he came the first time, a weary man and full of woes. The passion-flower yields us the best perfume, the tree of the cross bleeds the most healing balm. Like in this case cures like, for there is no remedy for sorrow beneath the sun like the sorrows of Immanuel. As Aaron's rod swallowed up all the other rods, so the griefs of Jesus make our griefs disappear. Thus you see that in the black soil of our subject light is sown for the righteous, light which springs up for those who sit in darkness and in the region of the shadow of death. Let us go, then, without reluctance to the house of mourning, and commune with 'The Chief Mourner,' who above all others could say, 'I am the man that hath seen the affliction.'

We will not stray from our text this morning, but keep to it so closely as even to dwell upon each one of its words. The words shall give us our divisions: - 'a man;' 'a man of sorrows;' 'acquainted with grief.'

A MAN

'A MAN.' There is no novelty to anyone here present in the doctrine of the real and actual manhood of the Lord Jesus Christ; but, although there be nothing novel in it, there is everything important in it, therefore, let us hear it again. This is one of those gospel church-bells which must be rung every Sabbath-day: this is one of those provisions of the Lord's household, which, like bread and salt, should be put upon the table at every spiritual meal. This is the manna which must fall every day round about the camp. We can never meditate too much upon Christ's blessed person as God and as man. Let us reflect that he who is here called a man was certainly 'very God of very God;' 'a man,' and 'a man of sorrows,' and yet at the same time, 'God over all, blessed for ever.' He who was 'despised and rejected of men' was beloved and adored by angels, and he from whom men hid their faces in contempt, was worshipped by cherubim and seraphim. This is the great mystery of godliness, God was 'manifest in the flesh.' He who was God, and was in the beginning with God, was made flesh, and dwelt among us. The Highest stooped to become the lowest, the Greatest took his place among the least. Strange, and needing all our faith to grasp it, yet it is true that he who sat upon the well of Sychar, and said 'Give me to drink,' was none other than he who digged the channels of the ocean, and poured into them the floods. Son of Mary, thou art also Son of Jehovah! Man of the substance of thy mother, thou art also essential Deity; we worship thee this day in spirit and in truth!

Remembering that Jesus Christ is God, it now behoves us to recollect that his manhood was none the less real and substantial. It differed from our own humanity in the absence of sin, but it differed in no other respect. It is idle to speculate upon a heavenly manhood, as some have done, who have, by their very attempt at accuracy, been borne down by whirlpools of error. It is enough for us to know that the Lord was born of a woman, wrapped in swaddling bands, laid in a manger, and needed to be nursed by his mother as any other little child; he grew in stature like any other human being, and as a man we know that he ate and drank, that he hungered and thirsted, rejoiced and sorrowed. His body could be touched and handled, wounded and made to bleed. He was no phantasm, but a man of flesh and blood, even as ourselves; a man needing sleep, requiring food, and subject to pain, and a man who, in the end, yielded up his life to death. There may have been some distinction between his body and ours, for inasmuch as it was never defiled by sin, it was not capable of corruption; otherwise in body and in soul, the Lord Jesus was perfect man after the order of our manhood, 'made in the likeness of

been under bondage to Satan will see in that same human nature an attraction leading them to approach him. Sinner, thou hast not to come to an absolute God, thou art not bidden to draw nigh to the consuming fire. Thou mightest well tremble to approach him whom thou hast so grievously offended; but, there is a man ordained to mediate between thee and God, and if thou wouldst come to God, thou must come through him, the man Christ Jesus. God out of Christ is terrible out of his holy places, he will by no means spare the guilty: - but look at yonder Son of man!

'His hand no thunder bears,
No terror clothes his brow;
No bolts to drive your guilty souls
To fiercer flames below.'

Here is a man with hands full of blessing, eyes wet with tears of pity, lips overflowing with love, and a heart melting with tenderness. See ye not the gash in his side? - through that wound there is a high-way to his heart, and he who needs his compassion may soon excite it. O sinners! the way to the Saviour's heart is open, and penitent seekers shall never be denied. Why should the most despairing be afraid to approach the Saviour? He has deigned to assume the character of the lamb of God, - I never knew even a little child that was afraid of a lamb; the most timorous will approach a lamb, and Jesus used this argument when he said to every labouring and heavy laden one, 'Take my yoke upon you, and learn of me, for I am meek and lowly in heart.' I know you feel yourselves sad and trembling, but need you tremble in HIS presence? If you are weak, your weakness will touch his sympathy, and your mournful inability will be an argument with his abounding mercy. If I were sick and might have my choice where I would lie, with a view to healing, I would say, place me where the best and kindest physician upon earth can see me, put me where a man with great skill, and equal tenderness, will have me always beneath his eye: I shall not long groan there in vain - if he can heal me he will. Sinner, place thyself by an act of faith this morning beneath the cross of Jesus and look up to him and say, 'Blessed Physician, thou whose wounds for me can heal me, whose death for me can make me live, look down upon me! Thou art man, thou knowest what man suffers. Thou art man, wilt thou let a man sink down to hell who cries to thee for help? Thou art a man, and thou canst save, and wilt thou let a poor unworthy one who longs for mercy be driven into hopeless misery, while he cries to thee to let thy merits save him?' Oh, ye guilty ones, have faith that ye can reach the heart of Jesus. Sinner, fly to Jesus without fear; he waits to save, it is his office to receive sinners and reconcile them to God. Be thankful that you have not to go to God at the first, and as you are, but you are invited to come to Jesus Christ, and through him to the Father. May the Holy Spirit lead you to devout meditation upon the humility of our Lord; and so may you find the door of life, the portal of peace, the gate of heaven!

Then let me add before I leave this point, that every child of God ought also to be comforted by the fact that our Redeemer is one of our own race, seeing that he was made like unto his brethren, that he might be a merciful and faithful High Priest; and he was tempted in all points, like as we are, that he might be able to succour them that are tempted. The sympathy of Jesus is the next most precious thing to his sacrifice. I stood by the bedside of a Christian brother the other day, and he remarked, 'I feel thankful to God that our Lord took our sicknesses.' 'Of course,' said he, 'the grand thing was, that he took our sins, but next to that, I, as a sufferer, feel grateful that he also took our sicknesses.' Personally, I also bear witness that it has been to me, in seasons of great pain, superlatively comfortable to know that in every pang which racks his people the Lord Jesus has a fellow-feeling. We are not alone, for one like unto the Son of man walks the furnace with us. The clouds which float over our sky have aforetime darkened the heavens for him also -

'He knows what strong temptations mean,
For he has felt the same.'

How completely it takes the bitterness out of grief to know that it once was suffered by him. The Macedonian soldiers, it is said, made long forced marches which seemed to go beyond the power of mortal endurance, but the reason for their untiring energy lay in Alexander's presence. He was accustomed to walk with them, and bear the like fatigue. If the king himself had been carried like a Persian monarch in a palanquin, in the midst of easy, luxurious state, the soldiers would soon have grown tired; but, when they looked upon the king of men himself, hungering when they hungered, thirsting when they thirsted, often putting aside the cup of water offered to him, and passing it to a fellow-soldier who looked more faint than himself, they could not dream of repining. Why every Macedonian felt that he could endure any fatigue if Alexander could. This day, assuredly, we can bear poverty, slander, contempt, or bodily pain, or death itself, because Jesus Christ our Lord has borne it. By his humiliation it shall become pleasure to be abased for his sake, by the spittle that distilled adown his cheeks it shall become a fair thing to be made a mockery for him, by the buffeting and the blind-folding it shall become an honour to be disgraced, and by the cross it shall become life itself to surrender life for the sake of such a cause and so precious a Master! May the man of sorrows now appear to us, and enable us to bear our sorrows cheerfully. If there be consolation anywhere, surely it is to be found in the delightful presence of the Crucified: 'A MAN shall be a hiding-place from the wind, and a covert from the tempest.'

A MAN OF SORROWS

We must pass on to dwell awhile upon the next words, 'a man of sorrows.' The expression is intended to be very emphatic, it is not 'a sorrowful man,' but 'a man of sorrows,' as if he were made up of sorrows, and they were constituent elements of his being. Some are men of pleasure, others men of wealth, but he was 'a man of sorrows.' He and sorrow might have changed names. He who saw him, saw sorrow, and he who would see sorrow, must look on him. 'Behold, and see,' saith he 'if there was ever sorrow like unto my sorrow which was done unto me.'

Our Lord is called the man of sorrows for PECULIARITY, for this was his peculiar token and special mark. We might well call him 'a man of

holiness;' for there was no fault in him: or 'a man of labours, for he did
his Father's business earnestly; or a man of eloquence,' for never man
spake like this man. We might right fittingly call him in the language of
our hymn, 'The man of love,' for never was there greater love than glowed
in his heart. Still conspicuous as all these and many other excellencies
were, yet we gazed upon Christ and been asked afterwards what was the
most striking peculiarity in him, we should have said his sorrows. The
various parts of his character were so singularly harmonious that no one
quality predominated, so as to become a leading feature. In his moral
portrait, the eye is perfect, but so also is the mouth; the cheeks are as
beds of spices, but the lips also are as lilies, dropping sweet-smelling
myrrh. In Peter, you see enthusiasm exaggerated at times into
presumption, and in John, love for his Lord would call fire from heaven
on his foes. Deficiencies and exaggerations exist everywhere but in Jesus.
He is the perfect man, a whole man, the holy one of Israel. But there was
a peculiarity, and it lay in the fact that 'his visage was so marred more
than any man, and his form more than the sons of men,' through the
excessive griefs which continually passed over his spirit. Tears were his
insignia, and the cross his escutcheon. He was the warrior in black
armour, and not as now the rider upon the white horse. He was the lord
of grief, the prince of pain, the emperor of anguish, a 'man of sorrows,
and acquainted with grief.'

> 'Oh! king of grief! (a title strange, yet true,
> To thee of all kings only due),
> Oh! king of wounds! how shall I grieve for thee,
> Who in all grief preventest me.'

Is not the title of 'man of sorrows' given to our Lord by way of
EMINENCE? He was not only sorrowful, but pre-eminent among the
sorrowful. All men have a burden to bear, but his was heaviest of all. Who
is there of our race that is quite free from sorrows? Search ye the whole
earth through, and everywhere the thorn and thistle will be found, and
these have wounded every one of woman born. High in the lofty places of
the earth there is sorrow, for the royal widow weeps her lord: down in the

cottage where we fancy that nothing but content can reign, a thousand bitter tears are shed over dire penury and cruel oppression. In the sunniest climes the serpent creeps among the flowers, in the most fertile regions poisons flourish as well as wholesome herbs. Everywhere 'men must work and women must weep.' There is sorrow on the sea, and sadness on the land. But in this common lot, the 'firstborn among many brethren' has more than a double portion, his cup is more bitter, his baptism more deep than the rest of the family. Common sufferers must give place, for none can match with him in woe. Ordinary mourners may be content to rend their garments, but he himself is rent in his affliction; they sip at sorrow's bowl, but he drains it dry. He who was the most obedient Son smarted most under the rod when he was stricken of God and afflicted; no other of the smitten ones have sweat great drops of blood, or in the same bitterness of anguish, cried, 'My God, my God, why hast thou forsaken me?'

The reasons for this superior sorrow may be found in the fact that with his sorrow there was no admixture of sin. Sin deserves sorrow, but it also blunts the edge of grief by rendering the soul untender and unsympathetic. We do not start at sin as Jesus did, we do not tremble at the sinner's doom as Jesus would. His was a perfect nature, which, because it knew no sin, was not in its element amid sorrow, but was like a land bird driven out to sea by the gale. To the robber the jail is his home, and the prison fare is the meat to which he is accustomed, but to an innocent man a prison is misery, and everything about it is strange and foreign. Our Lord's pure nature was peculiarly sensitive of any contact with sin; we, alas, by the fall, have lost much of that feeling. In proportion as we are sanctified, sin becomes the source of wretchedness to us; Jesus being perfect, every sin pained him much more than it would any of us. I have no doubt there are many persons in the world who could live merrily in the haunts of vice – could hear blasphemy without horror, view lust without disgust, and look on robbery or murder without abhorrence; but to many of us, an hour's familiarity with such abominations would be the severest punishment. A sentence in which the name of Jesus is blasphemed is torture to us of the most exquisite kind. The very mention of the shameful deeds of vice seizes us with horror. To live with the wicked would be a sufficient hell to the righteous. David's prayer is full of agony wherein he cries, 'Gather not my soul with sinners, nor my life with bloody men.' But the perfect Jesus, what a grief the sight of sin must have caused him! Our hands grow horny with toiling, and our hearts with sinning; but our Lord was, as it were, like a man whose flesh was all one quivering wound, he was delicately sensitive of every touch of sin. We go through thorn brakes and briars of sin because we are clothed with indifference, but imagine a naked man, compelled to traverse a forest of briars – and such was the Saviour, as to his moral sensitiveness. He could see sin where we cannot see it, and feel its heinousness as we cannot feel it: there was therefore more to grieve him, and he was more capable of being grieved.

Side by side with his painful sensitiveness of the evil of sin, was his gracious tenderness towards the sorrows of others. If we could know and enter into all the griefs of all of this congregation, it is probable that we should be of all men most miserable. There are heart-breaks in this house this morning, which, could they find a tongue, would fill our heart with agony. We hear of poverty here, we see disease there, we observe bereavement, and we mark distress, we note the fact that men are passing into the grave and, (ah, far more bitter grief,) descending into hell; but, somehow or other, either these become such common things, that they do not stir us, or else we gradually harden to them: the Saviour was always moved to sympathy with another's griefs, for his love was ever at flood-tide. All men's sorrows were his sorrows. His heart was so large, that it was inevitable that he should become 'a man of sorrows.'

We recollect that besides this our Saviour had a peculiar relationship to sin. He was not merely afflicted with the sight of it, and saddened by perceiving its effects on others, but sin was actually laid upon him, and he was himself numbered with the transgressors; and therefore he was called to bear the terrible blows of divine justice, and suffered unknown, immeasurable agonies. His Godhead strengthened him to suffer, else mere manhood had failed. The wrath whose power no man knoweth, spent itself on him; 'It pleased the Father to bruise him, he hath put him to grief.' Behold the man, and mark how vain it would be to seek his equal sorrow.

The title of 'man of sorrows,' was also given to our Lord to indicate
the CONSTANCY of his afflictions. He changed his place of abode, but he
always lodged with sorrow. Sorrow wove his swaddling bands, and sorrow
spun his winding sheet. Born in a stable, sorrow received him, and only
on the cross at his last breath did sorrow part with him. His disciples
might forsake him, but his sorrows would not leave him. He was often
alone without a man, but never alone without a grief. From the hour of his
baptism in Jordan, to the time of his baptism in the pains of death, he
always wore the sable robe and was 'a man of sorrows.'

He was also a 'a man of sorrows, ' for the VARIETY of his woes; he was a
man not of SORROW only, but of 'SORROWS.' All the sufferings of the body
and of the soul were known to him; the sorrows of the man who actively
struggles to obey; the sorrows of the man who sits still, and passively
endures. The sorrows of the lofty he knew, for he was the King of Israel;
the sorrows of the poor he knew, for he 'had not where to lay his head.'
Sorrows relative, and sorrows personal; sorrows mental, and sorrows
spiritual; sorrows of all kinds and degrees assailed him. Afflicted
emptied his QUIVER upon him, making his heart the target for all
conceivable woes. Let us think a minute or two of some of those sufferings.

Our Lord was a man of sorrows as to his poverty. Oh, you who are in
want, your want is not so abject as his: he had not where to lay his head,
but you have at least some humble roof to shelter you. No one denies you
a cup of water, but he sat upon the well at Samaria, and said, 'I thirst.' We
read more than once, that he hungered. His toil was so great that he was
constantly weary, and we read of one occasion where they took to him,
'even as he was,' into the ship – too faint was he to reach the boat
himself, but they carried him as he was and laid him down near the helm
to sleep; but he had not much time for slumber, for they woke him,
saying, 'Master, carest thou not that we perish:' a hard life was his, with
nothing of earthly comfort to make that life endurable.

Remember ye who lament around the open grave, or weep in memory
of graves but newly filled, our Saviour knew the heart-rendings of
bereavement. Jesus wept, as he stood at the tomb of Lazarus.

Perhaps the bitterest of his sorrows were those which were connected
with his gracious work. He came as the Messiah sent of God, on an

embassage of love, and men rejected his claims. When he went to his own city, where he had been brought up, and announced himself, they would have cast him headlong from the brow of the hill. It is a hard thing to come on an errand of disinterested love, and then to meet such ingratitude as this. Nor did they stay at cold rejection, they then proceeded to derision and to ridicule. There was no name of contempt, which they did not pour upon him; nay, it was not merely contempt, but they proceeded to falsehood, slander, and blasphemy. He was a drunken man, they said; hear this, ye angels, and be astonished! Yes, a wine-bibber did they call the blessed Prince of Life! They said he was in league with Beelzebub, and had a devil, and was mad; whereas he had come to destroy the works of the devil! They charged him with every crime which their malice could suggest. There was not a word he spoke but they would wrest it; not a doctrine but what they would misrepresent it: he could not speak but what they would find in his words some occasion against him. And all the while he was doing nothing but seeking their advantage in all ways. When he was earnest against their vices it was out of pity for their souls; if he condemned their sins it was because their sins would destroy them; but his zeal against sin was always tempered with love for the souls of men. Was there ever a man so full of good-will to others who received such disgraceful treatment from those he longed to serve?

As he proceeded in his life his sorrows multiplied. He preached, and when men's hearts were hard, and they would not believe what he said, 'he was grieved for the hardness of their hearts.' He went about doing good, and for his good works they took up stones again to stone him; alas, they stoned his heart when they could not injure his body. He pleaded with them, and plaintively declared his love, and received instead thereof a hatred remorseless and fiendish: slighted love has griefs of peculiar poignancy: many have died of hearts broken by ingratitude. Such love as the love of Jesus could not for the sake of those it loved bear to be slighted; it pined within itself because men did not know their own mercies and rejected their own salvation. His sorrow was not that men injured him, but that they destroyed themselves; this it was that pulled up the sluices of his soul, and made his eyes o'erflow with tears:

'O Jerusalem! Jerusalem! how often would I have gathered thy children together as a hen gathereth her chickens under her wings, and ye would not.' The lament is not for his own humiliation, but for their suicidal rejection of his grace. These were among the sorrows that he bore.

But surely he found some solace with the few companions whom he had gathered around him. He did; but for all that he must have found as much sorrow as solace in their company. They were dull scholars, they learned slowly; what they did learn they forgot, what they remembered they did not practise, and what they practised at one time they belied at another. They were miserable comforters for the man of sorrows. His was a lonely life, I mean that even when he was with his followers, he was alone. He said to them once, 'Could ye not watch with me one hour,' but indeed he might have said the same to them all the hours of their lives, for even if they sympathised with him to the utmost of their capacity, they could not enter into such griefs as his. A father in a house with many little children about him, cannot tell his babes his griefs; if he did they would not comprehend him. What know they of his anxious business transactions, or his crushing losses? Poor little things, their father does not wish they should be able to sympathise with him, he looks down upon them and rejoices that their toys will comfort them, and that their little prattle will not be broken in upon by his great griefs. The Saviour, from the very dignity of his nature, must suffer alone. The mountain-side with Christ upon it seems to me to be a suggestive symbol of his earthly life. His great soul lived in vast solitudes, sublime and terrible, and there amid a midnight of trouble , his spirit communed with the Father, no one being able to accompany him into the dark glens and gloomy ravines of his unique experience. Of all his life's warfare he might have said in some senses 'of the people there was none with me;' and at the last it became literally true, for they all forsook him – one denied him and another betrayed him, so that he trod the winepress alone.

In the last, crowning sorrows of his life, there came upon him the penal inflictions from God, the chastisement of our peace which was upon him. He was arrested in the garden of Gethsemane by God's officers before the officers of the Jews had come near to him. There on the ground he knelt, and wrestled till the bloody sweat started from every pore, and his soul was 'exceeding sorrowful, even unto death.' You have read the story of your Master's woes, and know how he was hurried from bar to bar; and treated with mingled scorn and cruelty before each judgement seat. When they had taken him to Herod and Pilate, and almost murdered him with scourging, they brought him forth, and said, ECCE HOMO – 'Behold the man.' Their malice was not satisfied, they must go further yet, and nail him to his cross, and mock him while fever parched his mouth and made him feel as if his body were dissolved to dust. He cries out, "I thirst;" and is mocked with vinegar. Ye know the rest, but I would have you best remember that the sharpest scourging and severest griefs were all within; while the hand of God bruised him, and the iron rod of justice broke him, as it were, upon the wheel.

He was fitly named a 'man of sorrows!' I feel as if I had no utterance, as if my tongue were tied, while trying to speak upon this subject. I cannot find goodly words worthy of my theme, yet I know that embellishments of language would degrade rather than adorn the agonies of my Lord. There let the cross stand sublime in its simplicity! It needs no decoration. If I had wreaths of choicest flowers to hang about it, I would gladly place them there, and if instead of garlands of flowers, each flower could be a gem of priceless worth, I would consider that the cross deserved the whole. But as I have none of these I rejoice that the cross alone, in naked simplicity, needs nought from mortal speech. Turn to your bleeding Saviour, O my hearers. Continue gazing upon him, and find in the 'man of sorrows' your Lord and your God.

ACQUAINTED WITH GRIEF

And now the last word is, he was 'ACQUAINTED WITH GRIEF.' With grief he had an INTIMATE acquaintance. He did not know merely what it was in others, but it came home to himself. We have read of grief, we have sympathised with grief, we have sometimes felt grief: but the Lord felt it more intensely than other men in his innermost soul; he , beyond us all, was conversant with this black letter lore. He knew the secret of the heart which refuseth to be comforted. He had sat at grief's table, eaten of grief's black bread, and dipped his morsel in her vinegar. By the waters of Marah he dwelt, and knew right well the bitter well. HE AND GRIEF WERE BOSOM FRIENDS.

It was a CONTINUOUS acquaintance. He did not call at grief's house sometimes to take a tonic by the way, neither did he sip now and then of the wormwood and the gall, but the QUASSIA CUP WAS ALWAYS HIS HAND, and ashes were always mingled with his bread. Not only forty days in the wilderness did Jesus fast; the world was ever a wilderness to him, and his life was one long Lent. I do not say that he was not, after all, a happy man, for down, deep in his soul, benevolence always supplied a living spring of joy to him. There was a joy into which we are one day to enter – the 'joy of our Lord' – the 'joy set before him' for which 'he endured the cross, despising the shame;' but that does not at all take away from the fact that his acquaintance with grief was continuous and intimate beyond that of any man who ever lived. It was indeed a GROWING acquaintance with grief, for each step took him deeper down into the grim shades of sorrow. As there is a progress in the teaching of Christ and in the life of Christ, so is there also in the griefs of Christ. The tempest lowered darker, and darker, and darker. His sun rose in a cloud, but it set in congregated horrors of heaped-up night, till in a moment, the clouds were suddenly rent in sunder, and, as a loud voice proclaimed, 'It is finished,' a glorious morning dawned where all expected an eternal night.

Remember once more that this acquaintance of Christ with grief was a VOLUNTARY acquaintance for our sakes. He need never have known a grief at all, and at any moment he might have said to grief, farewell. He could have returned in an instant to the royalties of heaven and to the bliss of the upper world, or even tarrying here he might have lived sublimely indifferent to the woes of mankind. But he would not, he remained to the end, out of love to us, grief's acquaintance.

Now, then, what shall I say in conclusion, but just this: let us admire the superlative love of Jesus. O love, love, what hast thou done! What hast thou not done! Thou art omnipotent in suffering. Few of us can bear pain, perhaps, fewer still of us can bear misrepresentation, slander, and ingratitude. These are horrible hornets which sting as with fire: men have been driven to madness by cruel scandals which have distilled from venomous tongues. Christ, throughout life, bore these and other sufferings. Let us love him, as we think of how much he must have loved us. Will you try this afternoon, before you come to the communion table, to get your souls saturated with the love of Christ? Lay them a-soak in his love all the afternoon, till like a sponge, ye drink into your own selves the love of Jesus; and then come up tonight, as it were, to let that love flow out to him again, while ye sit at his table and partake of the emblems of his death and of his love. Admire the power of his love, and then pray that you may have a love somewhat akin to it in power. We sometimes wonder why the church of God grows so slowly, but I do not wonder when I recollect what scant consecration to Christ there is in the church of God. Jesus was 'a man of sorrows, and acquainted with grief;' but many of his disciples who profess to be altogether his are living for themselves. There are rich men who call themselves saints, and are thought to be so, whose treasures are hoarded for themselves and families. There are men of ability who believe that they are bought with Christ's blood, yet their ability is all spent on other things and none upon their Lord. And let us come nearer home; here are we, what are we doing? Teaching in the school are you, - are you doing it with all your heart for Jesus? Preaching in the street? – yes, but do you throw your soul into it for him? Mayhap, you have to confess you are doing nothing; do not let this day conclude till you have begun to do something for your Lord. We are always talking about the church doing this and that, - what is the church? I believe there is a great deal too much said, both of bad and good, about that abstraction; the fact is, we are individuals. The church is only the aggregation of individuals, and if any good is to be done it must be performed by individuals, and if all individuals are idle there is no church work done; there may be the semblance of it, but there is no real work done. Brother, sister, what art thou doing for Jesus? I charge thee by the nail-prints of his hands, unless thou be a liar unto him, labour for him! I charge thee by his wounded feet – run to his help! I charge thee by the scar in his side – give him thy heart! I charge thee by that sacred head, once pierced with thorns, - yield him thy thoughts! I charge thee by the shoulders which bore the scourges, - bend thy whole strength to his service! I charge thee by himself, give him thyself. I charge thee by that left hand which has been under thy head, and that right hand which has embraced thee, by the roes and by the hinds of the field by the beds of spices, and the banquets of love, render thyself, thy heart, thy soul, and strength to him! Live in his service, and die in service! Lay not down thy harness, but work on as long as thou shalt live. Whilst thou livest let this be thy motto – 'All for Jesus, all for Jesus; all for the man of sorrows, all for the man of sorrows!' O ye that love him, and fight for him, you are summoned to the front. Hasten to the conflict, I pray you, and charge home for the 'man of sorrows!' Make this the battle-cry today! Slink not back like cowards! Hie not to your homes as lovers of ease! but press to the front for the 'man of sorrows,' like good men and true. By the cross which bore him, and by the heavy cross he bore, by his deadly agony, and by the agony of his life, I cry, 'forward, for the man of sorrows!' Write this word, "for the man of sorrows," on your own bodies, wherein ye bear the marks of the Lord Jesus; brand, if not in your flesh, yet in your souls, for henceforth ye are servants to the man of sorrows! Write this on your wealth, bind this inscription on all your possessions – 'This belongs to the man of sorrows.' Give your children to the 'man of sorrows,' as men of old consecrated their sons to patriotism, and to battle with their country's foes. Give up each hour to the 'man of sorrows!'. Learn even to eat and drink and sleep for the "man of sorrows," doing all in his name. Live for him and be ready to die for him, and the Lord accept you for the 'man of sorrows" sake. Amen.

❧ DWIGHT LYMAN MOODY

Dwight Lyman Moody (1837-1899) may well have been the greatest evangelist of all time. It was Henry Varley who said, 'It remains to be seen what God will do with a man who gives himself up wholly to Him' and D. L. Moody resolved to be, under God, that man.

In a forty year period he travelled more than a million miles and preached to more than one hundred million people. When asked on one occasion what was his creed, his reply was 'My creed is Isaiah 53.'

This message on the physical sufferings of Christ is from HOLDING THE FORT comprising sermons and addresses preached at the great revival meetings conducted by Moody and Sankey. It was published by Quaker City Publishing Co. Philadelphia, 1877.

Chapter four

THE PHYSICAL SUFFERINGS OF CHRIST

'SURELY HE HATH BORNE OUR GRIEFS, AND CARRIED OUR SORROWS: YET WE DID
ESTEEM HIM STRICKEN, SMITTEN OF GOD, AND AFFLICTED. BUT HE WAS WOUNDED
FOR OUR TRANSGRESSIONS, HE WAS BRUISED FOR OUR INIQUITIES: THE
CHASTISEMENT OF OUR PEACE WAS UPON HIM; AND WITH HIS STRIPES WE ARE
HEALED.' - ISAIAH 53:4-5

YOU WILL FIND MY TEXT THIS EVENING IN THE 53RD CHAPTER OF
ISAIAH, 4TH AND 5TH VERSES: 'SURELY HE HATH BORNE OUR
griefs, and carried our sorrows: yet we did esteem him stricken, smitten
of God, and afflicted. But he was wounded for our transgressions, he was
bruised for our iniquities: the chastisement of our peace was upon him;
and with his stripes we are healed.'

Five times that little word 'OUR' is used – OUR SORROWS, OUR GRIEFS, OUR
INIQUITIES, OUR TRANSGRESSIONS, and the chastisement of OUR PEACE – there is
a substitute for you! I would like, if I could, to make that 53rd chapter of
Isaiah real. I would like, if I could this evening, to bring before this
congregation, or to bring out this truth – what Christ has suffered
for each one of us. We take up the Bible, we read the account of His

crucifixion and death, how He suffered in agony, and we go away, lay the Bible down and think nothing more about it. I remember when the war was going on I would read about a great battle having been fought, where probably ten thousand men had been killed and wounded, and after reading the article I would lay the paper aside and forget all about it. At last I went into the army myself; I saw the dying men, I heard the groans of the wounded, I helped comfort the dying and bury the dead, I saw the scene in all its terrible realities. After I had been on the battle-field I could not read an account of a battle without it making a profound impression upon me. I wish I could bring before you in living colours the sufferings and death of Christ. I do not believe that there would be a dry eye here. I want to speak of His physical sufferings, for that I think we can get hold of. No man knows all that Christ suffered. Now, when a great man dies we are all anxious to get his last words, and if it is a friend, how we treasure up that last word, how we tell it to his friends, and we never tire talking to our loved ones of how he made his departure from the world.

Now, let us visit Calvary; let us bring the scene down to this present age; let us bring it right down here into this world this evening; or let us go back in our imagination to the time of Christ's crucifixion; let us imagine we are living in the city of Jerusalem instead of New York; let us take just the last Thursday He was there before He was crucified. Let us just imagine we are walking up one of the streets of Jerusalem. You will see a small body of men walking down the street; every one is running to see what the excitement is. As we get nearer we find that it is Jesus with His Apostles. We just walk down the street with them, and we see them stop and enter a very common-looking house. They go in and we enter also, and there we find Jesus sitting with the Apostles. You can see sorrow depicted upon His brow. His disciples see it but do not know what has caused His grief. We are told He was sorrowful unto death. As He was sitting there, He said to the twelve, 'One of you shall this night betray me.' Then each of them wondered if it was him of whom that Master spoke, and they said, 'Is it I?' Then Judas, the traitor, said, 'Is it I?' Jesus said it was. Christ said, 'Judas, what thou doest do quickly.' Then Judas got up and left the room. For three years he had been associated with the

Son of God. For three years he had sat at the feet of Jesus. For three years he had heard those words of sympathy and love fall from His lips. For three years he had been one of the faithful twelve. He had seen Him perform His wonderful miracles. He had heard the parables as they fell from the lips of Jesus. For three years he had been a member of that little band. So he got up and went out into the night, the darkest night that this world ever saw. He goes out of that guest chamber. You can hear him as he goes down those steps, off into the darkness and the blackness of the night. Then he went to the Sanhedrin and he said, 'I will make a bargain with you, I will sell Him cheap;' and there he betrayed his Master for thirty pieces of silver. That was a small amount. Men condemn him, but how many are selling Him for less than that? How many will give Him up for less than that? There are men who will sell Him for a little pleasure, and women for two or three hours in a ball-room.

You can hear the money being counted. He puts it into his pocket. He says, 'Give me a band of men and I will take you where He is.' It was then that Christ said those beautiful words. It was on that night that He said, 'Let not your hearts be troubled. I go to prepare a place for you; and if I go to prepare a place for you, I will come again, that where I am there ye may be also.' Instead of the disciples trying to cheer Him, He is trying to cheer them. He takes Peter, James, and John off from the rest, and then He withdraws from them about a stone's throw. Then He prayed to the Father. He that knew no sin was to bear all our sins. He who was as spotless as the angels of heaven was to suffer for us. From this lone spot His earnest prayers ascended to heaven. And while He is praying the Apostles fall asleep, for their eyes are heavy. Peter, James, and John were heavy with sleep. When He gets up from prayer He looks into the distance. He sees the men who are hunting for Him. They are looking around through the olive trees for some one. He well knows who they are looking for. He went up to this band of men and said, 'Whom seek ye?' And they said, 'We seek Jesus of Nazareth.' 'Well,' said Jesus, 'I am He.' There was something about that reply that terrified those men. They trembled and fell to the ground. Then at last Judas came up, and I don't know but he put his arms around His neck and kissed Him. When Judas had kissed Christ, the soldiers seized Him, for Judas had told the soldiers that when they saw him kiss a man that was Him. Those hands that had wrought so many wonderful miracles, those hands that had often been raised to bless the disciples, were bound. Then Peter takes his sword and cuts off the high priest's servant's ear. But Jesus healed the wound at once. He would not let the soldier suffer.

Then they take Him back to Jerusalem. He can see the soldiers and the populace mocking Him. When they take Him back they are summoned before the Sanhedrin. They lead Him before the Sanhedrin, and Annas is sent for. He is taken before Annas and Caiaphas; Christ is taken before the rulers of the Jews. There were seventy that belonged to that Sanhedrin. The law required that two witnesses must appear against a person on trial before he could be convicted. They secure false witnesses, who come and swear falsely. Then the high priest asked Jesus what it was that those men witnessed against Him, but He said nothing. Then the high priest asked Him a second time and said, 'Art Thou the Christ, the Son of the Blessed?' Jesus answered, 'I am, and ye shall see the Son of Man sitting on the right hand of power, and coming in the clouds of heaven.' Then the high priest said, 'What need we any further witnesses? Ye have heard the blasphemy from His own lips.' And the verdict came forth, 'He is guilty of death!' What a sentence! After a moment He was pronounced guilty of death. You can see one of those soldiers strike Him with the palm of his hand. Another spits in His face. Why, if I would spit in one of these people's faces you would be disgusted and get up and leave the hall. They not only struck Him, but they spit upon Him. They keep Him until morning. While they are keeping Him Peter is out in the Judgment Hall swearing that he never knew Him. They had all forsaken Him. Judas had already come back and thrown down the money which he had been paid for betraying innocent blood. He was about going out to hang himself.

About daylight they take Christ before Pilate. They are so eager for His blood that they cannot wait. By this time the city is filled with strangers from all parts of the country. They had heard that the Galilean prophet had been brought before the Sanhedrin, that they had condemned Him, and that He was to die the cruel death of the Cross, and all they had to do was to get Pilate's consent and they would then put Him out of the way. Pilate looked at Him and talked with Him, and then said, 'I find no fault in this man.' And they shouted, 'Why, if you chastise this man and let Him go, you will do wrong; He is a Galilean.' 'Why,' said Pilate, 'is He a Galilean?' And they told Pilate that He was brought up at Nazareth. When he heard that, glad to get rid of the responsibility, Pilate says, 'Then I will send Him to Herod.' There are a great many Roman soldiers keeping back the crowds in the streets, the same as our police on some great day. You can see the soldiers going before the crowd that has Jesus clearing the streets. Herod was glad when Jesus was brought into his presence, for he hoped that He would perform some miracles to gratify his curiosity. We are told that Herod's men of war set Him at naught. They dressed Him up, took some cast-off clothing of one of their kings, perhaps, and said, 'Hail, King of the Jews!' Then they came up and struck Him on the face. Oh! my friends, let us make this scene real today! He was bruised for our transgressions. He is your substitute and mediator.

After they had mocked Him they dressed Him up in His own garments and brought Him before Pilate. You can see the crowd around the judgment hall. They are ready to put Him to death. Pilate wanted to chastise Christ and release Him, and then deliver a prisoner to them. And they cried, 'Away with this man and release unto us Barabbas.'

They opened the prison door and let the prisoner out. Then Pilate thought of a way to save Him. He remembered that it was custom among the Jews that on a certain day one prisoner was to be released to them and go unpunished. So he said to the Jews, 'Which of these two prisoners shall I release, Jesus or Barabbas?' And when the chief priest found out what was going on, he went through the crowd and asked that Barabbas might be released. The governor was disappointed, and when he put the question to the crowd, 'Which shall I release unto you, Jesus or Barabbas?' – Jesus who raised the dead, or Barabbas who took the lives of men – whose hands were dripping with the blood of his fellow-men? No sooner was it put to the crowd, than they lifted up their voices shouting, 'Barabbas, Barabbas!' Then said he, 'What shall I do with Jesus?' And the cry rang through the streets, 'Let Him be crucified!' But a few days before the crowd was crying, 'Hosanna to the Son of David!' Then, when the governor heard it he turned and wrung his hands saying, 'I am innocent of the blood of this just man.'

Oh, until I came to read about what Christ suffered, I never before realised what He had done for us. I never knew until I came to read about all the Roman custom of scourging what it meant by Christ being scourged for me. When I first read about that I threw myself on the floor and wept, and asked Him to forgive me for not having loved Him more. Let us imagine the scene where He is taken by the Roman soldiers to be scourged. The orders were to put forty stripes, one after another, upon His bared back. Sometimes it took fifteen minutes, and the man died in the process of being scourged. See Him stooping while the sins of the world are laid upon Him, and the whips come down upon His bare back, cutting clear through the skin and flesh to the bone. And, after they had scourged Him, instead of bringing oil and pouring it into the wounds, He who came to bind up the broken heart and pour oil into its wounds, instead of doing this they dressed Him up again, and some cruel wretch reached out to Him a crown of thorns, which was placed upon His brow. The Queen of England wears a crown of gold, filled with diamonds and precious stones, worth $20,000,000; but when they came to crown the Prince of Heaven, they gave Him a crown of thorns and placed them upon His brow, and in His hand they put a stick for a sceptre.

Now you might have seen at one of the gates of the city a great crowd bursting through. What is coming? There are two thieves being brought for execution. Between the two thieves is the Son of God, walking through the streets of Jerusalem. And He carried a cross. You ladies wear small crosses made of gold and wood and stone around your necks; but the cross that the Son of God carried was a rude, heavy tree, made into a cross. I can imagine Him reeling and staggering under it. Undoubtedly He had lost so much blood that He was too faint to carry it, and before they got to the place it well nigh crushed Him to the earth. And then some stranger undertook to bear it along after Him. I can imagine the strong man carrying it along, and the crowd hooting, 'Away with Him; away with Him' – a pestilent fellow, as they called Him. This was only nine o'clock in the morning. They arrived at Calvary a little before nine. Then they took up the Son of God and they laid Him out upon that cross. I can imagine then binding His wrists to the arms of the cross. After they had got Him bound, up came a soldier with a hammer and nails and put one nail into the palm of His hand, and then came the hammer without mercy, driving it down through the bone and flesh into the wood; and then into the other hand. And then they brought a long nail for His feet; and then the soldiers gathered round the cross and lifted it up, and the whole weight of the Son of God came upon those nails in His hands and feet. O, you young ladies, who say you see no beauty in Christ that you should desire to be like Him, come with me and take a look at those wounds, and remember that that crown of thorns was laid upon His brow by a mocking world. Look at Him as He hangs there, and at the people who pass by deriding Him. There are the two thieves that reviled Him, and the one that said, 'Save us and save Thyself if thou beest the Son of God.' But hark! At last there comes a cry from the cross. What is it? Is it a cry to the Lord to take Him down from the cross? No! It is 'Father, forgive them, for they know not what they do.' Was there ever such love as that? While they were crucifying Him He was lifting up His heart to God in prayer. His heart seemed to be breaking for those sinners. How He wanted to take them in His arms! How He wanted to forgive them! At last He cried, 'I thirst;' and instead of giving Him a draught of water from the spring, they gave Him a draught of gall mixed with vinegar. There He hung! You can see those soldiers casting lots for His garments as they crowd around the foot of the cross. While they were casting lots the crowd would mock and deride Him and make all manner of sport of Him. He cried only, 'Father, forgive them, for they know not what they do.'

Right in the midst of the darkness and gloom there came a voice from one of those thieves. It flashed into His soul as He hung there, 'This must be more than man; this must be the true Messiah!' He cried out, 'Lord, remember me when Thou comest into Thy Kingdom!' We are anxious to get the last word or act of our dying friends. Here was the last act of Jesus. He snatched the thief from the jaws of death, saying, 'This day shalt thou be with me in Paradise.' And again He spoke. What was it? 'It is finished,' was His cry. Salvation was wrought out, atonement was made. His blood had been shed; His life had been given. Undoubtedly, if we had been there, we would have seen legions of devils hovering around the cross. And so the dark clouds of death and hell came surging up against the bosom of the Son of God, and He drove them back as you have seen the waves come gathering up and surging against the rock, and then receding and then returning. The billows were over Him. He was conquering death and Satan and the world in those last moments. He was treading the wine-press alone. At last He shouted from the cross, "It is finished.' Perhaps no one who heard it knew what it meant. But the angels in heaven knew; and I can imagine the bells of Heaven (if they do have bells there) ringing out and the angels singing, 'The God-Man is dead,' and full restitution has opened the way back into Paradise, and all man has to do is to look and live." After He cried, 'It is finished,' He bowed His head, commended His spirit to God, and gave up the ghost. Do you tell me you see no reason why you should love such a Saviour? Would you rather be His enemy than His friend? Have you no desire to receive Him and become His? May God soften all our hard hearts today.

❦ THOMAS DeWITT TALMAGE

Thomas DeWitt Talmage (1832-1902). If Charles Spurgeon was the 'Prince of Preachers' then Thomas DeWitt Talmage must be recognised as one of the princes of the American pulpit. Spurgeon said of Talmage's ministry, 'His sermons take hold of my innermost soul. The Lord is with this mighty man. I am astonished when God blesses me, but not when He blesses him.'

He was the founding editor of THE CHRISTIAN HERALD and his sermons appeared in three thousand newspapers and magazines a week and he is said to have had twenty-five million readers.

For twenty-five years Talmage, a Presbyterian, filled the five thousand seats of the auditorium in his Brooklyn Church. This sermon is taken from TALMAGE'S SERMONS (vol.3).

Chapter five

LOST SHEEP

'ALL WE LIKE SHEEP HAVE GONE ASTRAY; WE HAVE TURNED EVERY ONE TO HIS OWN WAY; AND THE LORD HATH LAID ON HIM THE INIQUITY OF US ALL.' - ISAIAH 53:6

WITHIN NINETY YEARS AT THE VERY LONGEST THIS ENTIRE AUDIENCE WILL BE IN ETERNITY. DURING THE NEXT FIFTY YEARS you will nearly all be gone. The next ten years will cut a wide swathe among the people. The year 1882 will to some be the finality. This may be THE LAST SERMON that some one will hear. Under these circumstances, while I have a somewhat poetic nature, might indulge in trope and figure and simile, I dare not do so. God never gave to any man a greater fondness for mirth than I naturally have, and yet under this solemnity I would not dare indulge it. This service, this hour in spiritual things, will be to some in this assemblage a life-struggle or a death-grapple.

ONE

The first half of my text is an indictment.

'All we like sheep have gone astray.' Some one says, 'Can't you drop that first word? That is too general; that sweeps too great a circle.' Some man rises in the audience, and he looks over on the opposite side of the house and says, 'There is a BLASPHEMER, and I understand how HE has gone astray. And in another part of the house is a DEFAULTER, and HE has gone astray. And there is an IMPURE PERSON, and HE has gone astray.' Sit down, my brother, and look at home. My text takes us all in. It starts behind the pulpit, sweeps the circuit of the room, and comes back to the point where it started, when it says, 'ALL we like sheep have gone astray.'

I can very easily understand why Martin Luther threw up his hands after he had found the Bible, and cried out, 'Oh, my sins, my sins,' and why the publican, according to the custom to this day in the East, when they have any great grief, began to beat himself and cry as he smote upon his breast, 'God be merciful to me a sinner.'

I was brought up in the country, like many of you, and I know some of the habits of sheep, and how they get astray, and what my text means when it says, 'All we like sheep have gone astray.' SHEEP GET ASTRAY IN TWO WAYS: either by trying to get into other pastures, or from being scared by the dogs. In the former way some of us get astray. We thought the religion of Jesus Christ short commons. We thought there was better pasturage somewhere else. We thought if we could only lie down on the banks of distant streams, or under great oaks on the other side of some hill, we might be better fed. We wanted other pasturage than that which God through Jesus Christ gave our soul, and we wandered on, and we wandered on, and we were lost. WE WANTED BREAD AND WE FOUND GARBAGE. The further we wandered, instead of finding rich pasturage, we found blasted heath and sharper rocks and more stinging nettles but no pasture.

How was it in THE CLUB-HOUSE when you lost your child? Did they come around and help you very much? Did your worldly associates console you very much? Did not the plain Christian man who came to your house and sat up with your darling child give you more comfort than all worldly associations? Did all the convivial songs you ever heard comfort you in that day of bereavement so much as the song they sang to you, perhaps the very song that was sung by your little child the last Sabbath afternoon of her life?

'There is a happy land, far, far, away,
Where saints immortal reign, bright, bright as day.'

Did your business associates in that day of darkness and trouble give you any especial condolence? Business exasperated you, business wore you out, business left you limp as a rag, business made you mad. You got money, but you got no peace. God have mercy on the man who has nothing but business to comfort him! The world afforded you no luxuriant pasturage.

A famous English actor stood on the stage impersonating, and thunders of applause came down from the galleries, and many thought it was the proudest moment of his life; but there was a man asleep just in front of him and the fact that that man was indifferent and somnolent spoiled all the occasion for him, and he cried, 'Wake up, wake up!' So one little annoyance in your life has been more pervading to your mind than all the brilliant congratulations and success.

Poor pasturage for your soul you found in this world. The world has cheated you, the world has belied you, the world has misinterpreted you, the world has persecuted you. It never comforted you. O! this world is a good rack from which a horse may pick his food; it is a good trough from which the swine may crunch their mess; but it gives but little food to a soul blood-bought and immortal.

What is a soul? It has a hope high as the throne of God. What is a man? You say, 'It is only a man.' It is only a man gone overboard in sin. It is only a man gone overboard in his business life. What is a man? The battle ground of THREE WORLDS, with his hands taking hold of destinies of light or darkness. A man! No line can measure him. No limit can bound him. The archangel before the throne cannot outlive him. The stars shall die, but he will watch their extinguishment. The world will burn, but he will gaze on the conflagration. Endless ages will march on, he will watch the procession. A man! The masterpiece of God Almighty. Yet you say, 'It is only a man.' Can a nature like that be fed on husks of the wilderness?

'Substantial comfort will not grow
On nature's barren soil;
All we can boast till Christ we know
Is vanity and toil.'

Some of you got astray by looking for better pasturage; others by
being scared by the dogs.

The hound gets over into the pasture field. The poor sheep fly in
every direction. In a few moments they are torn in the hedges and they are
plashed in the ditch, and the lost sheep never gets home unless the farmer
goes after it. There is nothing so thoroughly lost as a lost sheep.

It may have been in 1857, during the financial panic or during the
financial stress in the fall Of 1873 when you got astray. You almost became
an atheist. You said, 'Where is God, that honest men go down and thieves
prosper?' You were dogged by creditors, you were dogged by the
banks, you were dogged by worldly disaster, and some of you went into
misanthropy, and some of you took to strong drink, and others fled out of
Christian association, and you got astray. Oh man! That was the last time
when you ought to have forsaken God. Standing amid the floundering of
your earthly fortunes, how could you get along without a God to comfort
you, and a God to deliver you, and a God to help you, and a God to save
you!

You tell me you have been through enough business trouble almost to
kill you. I know it. I cannot understand how the boat could live one hour
in that chopped sea. But I do not know by what process you got astray;
some in one way and some in another, and if you could really see the
position some of you occupy before God today your soul would burst
into agony of tears, and you would address the heavens with the cry, 'God
have mercy!' Sinai's batteries have been unlimbered above your soul, and
at times you have heard it thunder, 'The wages of sin is death.' 'All have
sinned and come short of the glory of God.' 'By one man sin entered into
the world, and death by sin; and so death passed upon all men, for that
all have sinned.' 'The soul that sinneth, it shall die.'

When Sebastopol was being bombarded in 1855, TWO RUSSIAN FRIGATES
burned all night in the harbour, throwing a glare upon the trembling

fortress; and some of you, from what you have told me yourselves, some of you are standing in the night out of your soul's trouble; the cannonade and the conflagration and the multiplication and the multitude of your sorrows and troubles I think must make the wings of God's hovering angels shiver to the tip.

TWO

But the last part of my text opens a divine door wide enough to let us all out and to let all heaven in. Sound it on the organ with all the stops out. Thrum it on the harps with all the tunes astring. With all the melody possible let the heavens sound it to the earth, and let the earth tell it to the heavens. 'The Lord hath laid on Him the iniquity of us all.' I am glad that the prophet did not stop to explain whom he meant by 'Him.' Him of the manger, Him of the bloody sweat, Him of the resurrection throne, Him of the crucifixion agony. 'On Him the Lord hath laid the iniquity of us all.'

'Oh!' says some man, 'that isn't generous, that isn't fair; let every man carry his own burden, and pay his own debts.' That sounds reasonable. If I have an obligation and I have the means to meet it, and I come to you and ask you to settle that obligation, you rightly say, 'Pay your own debts.' If you and I are walking down the street both hale, hearty, and well, and I ask you to carry me, you say and say rightly ' walk on your own feet!' But suppose you and I were in a regiment and I was wounded in the battle and fell unconscious at your feet with gunshot fractures and dislocations, what would you do? You would call to your comrades saying, 'Come and help; this man is helpless; bring the ambulance; let us take him to the hospital;' and I would be a dead lift in your arms, and you would lift me from the ground where I had fallen and put me in an ambulance, and take me to the hospital and have all kindness shown me. Would there be anything mean in your doing that? Would there be anything bemeaning in my accepting that kindness? Oh! no. You would be mean not to do it.

THAT IS WHAT CHRIST DOES. If we could pay our debts then it would be
better to go and pay them, saying, 'Here, Lord, here is my obligation;
here are the means with which I mean to settle that obligation; now give
me a receipt; cross it all out.' The debt is paid. But the fact is that we have
fallen in the battle. We have gone down under the hot fire of our
transgressions, we have been wounded by the sabres of sin, we are
helpless, we are undone. Christ comes. The loud clang heard in the sky
on that Christmas night was only the bell – the resounding bell of the
ambulance. Clear the way for the Son of God. He comes down to bind up
the wounds, and to scatter the darkness, and to save the lost. Clear the
way for the Son of God. Christ comes down to us, and we are a dead lift.
He does not lift us with the tips of His fingers. He does not lift us with
one arm. He comes down upon His knee and then with a dead lift He
raises us to honour and glory and immortality, 'The Lord hath laid on Him
the iniquity of us all.' Then will no man carry his sins? You cannot carry
successfully the smallest sin you ever committed. You might as well put
the Appennines on one shoulder and the Alps on the other – how much
less can you carry all the sins of your life-time? Christ comes and looks
down in your face and says, 'I have come through all the lacerations of
these days, and through all the tempests of these nights; I have come to
bear your burdens and to pardon your sins and to pay your debts. Put
them on My shoulder – put them on My heart.' 'On Him the Lord hath
laid the iniquities of us all.'

Sin has almost pestered the life out of some of you. At times it has
made you cross and unreasonable, and it has spoiled the brightness of
your days and the peace of your nights. There are men who have been
riddled of sin. The world gives them no solace. Gossamery and volatile
the world, while as they look forward to it eternity is black as midnight.
They writhe under the stings of a conscience which proposes to give no
rest here, and no rest hereafter, and yet they do not repent, they do not
pray, they do not weep. They do not realise that just the portion they
occupy is the position occupied by scores, hundreds, and of men who
never found any hope. They went out of life just as they are now. They sat
in the same place where you sit, then they heard the Gospel call, they
rejected it, they passed out of life, and their voice comes to us from the

eternal world this morning, saying, 'Take the Gospel; this is your chance; my day is gone; I am undone! Who will push back this bolt? Who will put down this sorrow?' And the caverns forlornly echo, 'Who, who?'

If this meeting should be thrown open and the people who are here could give their testimony, what thrilling experiences we should hear on all sides! There is a man in the gallery who would say: 'I had brilliant surroundings, I had the best education that one of the best collegiate institutions of this country could give, and I observed all the moralities of life, and I was self-righteous, and I thought I was all right before God as I am all right before men; but the Holy Spirit came to me one day and said, 'You are a sinner;' the Holy Spirit persuaded me of the fact. While I had escaped the sins against the law of the land, I had really committed the worst sin a man ever commits – the driving back of the Son of God, from my heart's affections. And I saw that my hands were red with the blood of the Son of God, and I began to pray, and peace came to my heart, and I know by experience that what you say this morning is true. 'On Him the Lord hath laid the iniquity of us all.'

Yonder is a man who would say: 'I was the worst drunkard in New York; I went from bad to worse; I destroyed myself, I destroyed my home; my children cowered when I entered the house; when they put up their lips to be kissed I struck them; when my wife protested against the mal-treatment, I treated her with cruelty and unkindness. I know all the bruises and all the terrors of a drunkard's woe. I went on further and further from God until one day I got a letter saying: 'MY DEAR HUSBAND: I have tried every way, done everything, and prayed earnestly and fervently for your reformation, but it seems of no avail. Since our little Henry died, with the exception of those few happy weeks when you remained sober, my life has been one of sorrow. Many of the nights I have sat by the window, with my face bathed in tears, watching for your coming. I am broken-hearted, I am sick. Mother and father have been here frequently and begged me to come home, but my love for you and my hope for brighter days have always made me refuse them. That hope seems now beyond realisation, and I have returned to them. It is hard, and I battled long before doing it. May God bless and preserve you, and take from you that accursed appetite and hasten the day when we shall be

again living happily together. This will be my daily prayer, knowing that
He has said: 'Come unto me all ye that labour and are heavy laden, and I
will give you rest.' From your loving wife, MARY.'

'And so I wandered on and on,' says that man, 'until one night I passed
a Methodist meeting-house, and I said to myself, 'I'll go in and see what
they are doing,' and I got to the door, and they were singing:

'All may come, whoever will,
This Man receives poor sinners still.'

'And I dropped right there where I was and I said, "God have mercy,"
and He had mercy on me. My home is restored, my wife sings all day long
during work, my children come out a long way to greet me home, and my
household is a little heaven. I will tell you what did all this for me. It was
the truth that this day you proclaim: 'On Him the Lord hath laid the
iniquity of us all."

Yonder is a woman who would say: 'I wandered off from my father's
house: I heard the storm that pelts on a lost soul; my feet were blistered
on the hot rocks. I went on and on, thinking that no one cared for my
soul, when one night Jesus met me and He said, 'Poor thing, go home!
your father is waiting for you; your mother is waiting for you. Go home,
poor thing!' and, sir, I was too weak to pray, and I was too weak to repent,
but I just cried out, I sobbed out my sins and my sorrows on the
shoulders of Him of whom it is said: 'The Lord hath laid on Him the
iniquity of us all."

There is here a young man who would say: 'I had a Christian parentage
and bringing up: I came from the country to city life; I started well; I
had a good position, a good commercial position, but one night AT THE
THEATRE I met some young men who did me no good. They dragged me all
through the sewers of iniquity, and I lost my morals, and I lost my
position, and I was shabby and wretched. I was going down the street,
thinking that no one cared for me, when a young man tapped me on the
shoulder and said: "George come with me and I will do you good." I
looked at him to see whether he was joking or not. I saw he was in
earnest, and I said: "What do you mean, sir?" "Well," he replied "I mean

if you come to the meeting tonight, I will be very glad to introduce you. I will meet you at the door. Will you come?" I said, "I will," and went.

'I went to the place where I was lodging. I buttoned my coat over a ragged vest and went to the door of the church, and the young man met me, and we went in; and as I went in I heard an old man praying, and he looked so much like my old father, I sobbed right out, and they were all around so kind and sympathetic that I just there gave my heart to God; and I know this morning, that what you say is truth; I believe it in my own experience. "On Him the Lord hath laid the iniquity of us all."

Oh! my brother, without stopping to look as to whether your hands tremble or not, without stopping to look whether your face is bloated with sin or not, let me give you one warm, brotherly Christian grip, and invite you right up to the heart, to the compassion, to the sympathy, to the pardon of Him on whom the Lord hath laid the iniquity of us all. Throw away your sins. Carry them no longer. I proclaim emancipation this morning to all who are bound, pardon for all sin, and eternal life for all the dead.

Some one comes here this morning, and I stand aside. He comes up these steps. He comes to this place. I must stand aside. Taking that place He spreads abroad His hands, as they were nailed. You see His feet, they were bruised. He pulls aside the robe and shows you His wounded heart. I say, 'Art Thou weary?' 'Yes,' He says, 'weary with the world's woe.' I say, 'Whence camest Thou?' He says, 'I come from Calvary.' I say, 'Who comes with Thee?' He says, 'No one; I have trodden the winepress alone.' I say, 'Why comest Thou here?' 'Oh!' He says, 'I came here to carry all the sins and sorrows of the people.' And He kneels and He says: 'Put on my shoulders all the sorrows and all the sins.' And conscious of my own sins, first, I take them and put them on the shoulders of the Son of God.

I say: 'Canst Thou bear any more, O Christ?' He says, 'Yea, more.' And I gather up all the sins of all those who serve at these altars, the officers of the Church of Jesus Christ – I gather up all their sins and I put them on Christ's shoulders, and I say: 'Canst Thou bear any more?' He says, 'Yea, more.' Then I gather up all the sins a hundred people in this house and I put them on the shoulders of Christ, and I say: 'Canst Thou bear more?' He says, 'Yea, more.' And I gather up all the sins of this assembly and I put them on the shoulders of the Son of God and I say: 'Canst Thou bear them?' 'Yea,' He says, 'more.'

But HE IS DEPARTING. Clear the way for Him, the Son of God. Open the door and let Him pass out. He is carrying our sins and bearing them away. We shall never see them again. He throws them down into the abysm, and you hear the long reverberating echo of their fall. 'On Him the Lord hath laid the iniquity of us all.' Will you let Him take your sins today? or do you say, 'I will take charge of them myself, I will fight my own battles, I will risk eternity on my own account?' O! brother, then you will perish. I know not how near some of you have come to crossing the line.

A clergyman said in his pulpit one Sabbath: 'Before next Saturday night one of this audience will have passed out of life.' A gentleman said to another seated next to him: 'I don't believe it; I mean to watch, and if it doesn't come true by next Saturday night, I shall tell that that clergyman his falsehood.' The man seated next to him said: 'Perhaps it will be yourself.' 'O! no,' the other replied, 'I shall live to be an old man.' That night he breathed his last.

Today, the Saviour calls. All may come. GOD NEVER PUSHES A MAN OFF. God never destroys anybody. The man jumps off, he jumps off. It is suicide – soul suicide – if the man perishes, for the invitation is, 'Whosoever will let him come.' Whosoever, whosoever, whosoever!

There may be in this audience just one man who will reject the Gospel. It seems to me that the vast multitude will see that the Gospel is reasonable and they will surrender themselves to God; but there may be in this house just one who will refuse the Gospel, and pass out and pass down. Let me take some solemn leave of such an one. Watch cautiously your health, for when your life ceases here all pleasant experiences cease. Walk not near the scaffolding lest a brick or a stone should fall and you should be ushered into a world for which you have no preparation. Tomorrow morning you will go over to the shop, or the bank, or the factory, and they will say: 'Where were you on the Sabbath?' You will say, 'I was at the Tabernacle and I heard the Gospel preached; there were some things in the sermon I didn't believe, I could not receive, I could not accept.' And so the days will go by, and the hours and the moments until after a while eternity will rush upon you. I am speaking to just that one soul. Farewell, thou doomed spirit! As thou shovest off from hope I waive thee this salutation. O! it is hard to part for ever. I bid thee a long, a last, a bitter, an eternal adieu!

'While God invites, how blest the day,
How sweet the Gospel's charming sound;
Come, sinner, haste, oh, haste away,
While yet a pardoning God is found.'

In this day of merciful visitation, while many are coming into the kingdom of God, join the procession Heavenward.

Seated here during the last service we had was a man who came in and said: 'I don't know that there is any God.' That was on Friday night. I said: 'We will kneel down and find out whether there is any God.' And in the second seat from the pulpit we knelt. He said: 'I have found Him. There is a God, a pardoning God. I feel Him here.' He knelt in the darkness of sin. He arose two minutes afterwards in the liberty of the Gospel; while another sitting under the gallery on Friday night said: 'My opportunity is gone; last week I might have been saved, not now; the door is shut.' And another from the very midst of the meeting, during the week, rushed out of the front door of the Tabernacle, saying 'I am a lost man.'

'Behold! The Lamb of God who taketh away the sin of the world.' 'Now is the accepted time. Now is the day of salvation.' 'It is appointed unto all men once to die, and after that – the judgment!'

❦ ALAN REDPATH

Alan Redpath was born in 1907, in Gosforth, Newcastle-upon-Tyne, England. He came to know the Lord Jesus Christ as his Saviour through the witness of a business colleague in August 1926.

In 1936, he felt the Lord directing him to leave his job as an accountant, and he joined the staff of the National Young Life Campaign, where he remained as an evangelist for four years. In 1940 he received and accepted a call to the pastorate of Duke Street Baptist Church in Richmond, London.

In 1953 he moved to Moody Memorial Church in Chicago, where he served as pastor until 1962. He returned to Great Britain in November of that year, and assumed the responsibility of the pastorate of Charlotte Baptist Chapel in Edinburgh, Scotland, where he remained until 1966. This sermon is taken from the book, 'SERMONS FOR TODAY' edited by A. H. Chapple.

Chapter six

WHEN SILENCE IS GOLDEN

'HE WAS OPPRESSED, AND HE WAS AFFLICTED, YET HE OPENED NOT HIS MOUTH:
HE IS BROUGHT AS A LAMB TO THE SLAUGHTER, AND AS A SHEEP BEFORE HER
SHEARERS IS DUMB, SO HE OPENETH NOT HIS MOUTH.' — ISAIAH 53:7

ONE TRANSLATION RENDERS THIS VERSE, 'HE WAS HARD PRESSED
AND HUMBLED HIMSELF, YET HE OPENED NOT HIS MOUTH.'
Here is the attitude of the Saviour in the face of suffering, and the
repetition of those words suggests the pre-eminent thing in His attitude
was silence. Never man spoke like this Man, but never man was silent like
Him.

Recall the last moments of our Lord's life here on earth, when all hell
was let loose upon Him.

a) Before Caiaphas (Matthew 26:62-64).

Here He stands before the High Priest, accused of blasphemy. He is
silent, except when to remain silent would have been to deny His claim to
deity.

b) Before Pilate (Matthew 27:11-14).

Here He stands before the Roman Governor, accused of treason. He is silent, except when to remain so would have been to deny His claim to kingship.

c) Before the whole band of soldiers, who stripped Him, crowned Him with thorns, blindfolded Him, spat on Him, smote Him with a reed, struck Him in the face and mocked Him, not a single word crossed His lips.

In view of this silence we must remember that in the Garden of Gethsemane one word from Him, one brief glimpse of His power, had caused those sent to arrest Him to fall on their faces to the ground. But at His infamous trial He restrains His omnipotence. One glance to heaven, and the earth could have opened to swallow all who opposed Him.

What a tremendous display of power was revealed in the silence which restrained Him in the face of the scorn of His enemies!

d) Before Herod (Luke 23:8-9).

Questioned regarding many things, yet He answered not a word to the man who had sinned away his opportunity and forfeited every claim upon the salvation of God. There is a terrifying possibility of someone to sit under a Biblical ministry, to sense conviction, yet to refuse to forsake sin. To such Jesus is silent.

e) At Calvary (Matthew 27:45-46).

Darkness and silence reigned for three long hours. Hell did its worst, letting loose all its fury. Yet the Lord was silent, until the ninth hour when the silence was broken by that awesome cry, 'My God, My God, why hast Thou forsaken Me?'

Yes, the pre-eminent thing about His suffering was His silence. Before all His accusers and tormentors He spoke not one word of complaint, only of testimony. Never did He speak to plead His innocence, only to claim His authority. Truly, He was hard pressed and humbled Himself, yet He opened not His mouth. He is brought as a lamb to the slaughter, and as a sheep before her shearers is dumb, so He opened not His mouth.

We can only bow in wonder and worship, and ask, why the silence? The answer of the world is in Isaiah 53:4b, that He must be guilty of all that was charged against Him, otherwise a loving God would not have allowed it to happen. But we cannot accept that explanation; the whole revelation of Scripture contradicts it.

What, then, does it mean? In seeking to answer that question we do so not merely to understand His silence in its bearing upon His life and testimony, but also to recognise its message for our own hearts. The Cross has a twofold implication. It spells redemption from sin, but also, and as a sequel to that redemption, identification with the One who suffered on it in displaying the whole principle of Christian living to others. This is the meaning of Galatians 2:20.

In some aspects He was unique, yet I can learn from the silence of Jesus when silence is golden in my own experience also.

I   THE SILENCE OF DECISIVENESS IN COMMITMENT TO THE WILL OF GOD.

Turn to two New Testament verses: He was delivered by the determinate counsel and foreknowledge of God (Acts 2:23). My meat is to do the will of Him that sent Me, and to finish His work (John 4:34).

Does not His silence declare the refusal to utter one word to prevent His death, for He was committed to the will of God to be a sacrifice for us. So entirely and decisively was He surrendered that He would not interfere in His own behalf, even in the slightest degree, but rather consented to be bound and slain without struggle and without complaint. There was no reserve: body, soul and spirit were wholly given up to the Father's will. Not one faculty He possessed asked to be excused. Every limb of His body, every thought of His mind, every desire of His spirit was in submission. It was a whole Christ giving up His whole being to God that He might offer Himself without spot for our redemption.

Oh, that your commitment and mine to His will were as decisive as that! To resign ourselves completely, to deliver up our lives in their entirety in self-conquest to God; to find ourselves absorbed in one desire for His will; to see the sacrifice accepted, as was Elijah's on Mount Carmel, and to have the answering fire from heaven

'Burn up the dross of base desire,
And make the mountain flow!'

when the fire consumed not only the bullock and the wood, but licked up the water in the trench, and the whole sacrifice went up to heaven in one cloud of fire and smoke, a whole burnt-offering to the living God. Oh, that He would do that for us today, and settle forever our arguments and disputes concerning our right to ourselves! What right have we, in the light of Jesus refusing His own? In the furnishings of the Tabernacle are included flesh-hooks, which were used to keep the sacrifice upon the flame until it was reduced to a heap of ashes. The Christian too needs 'flesh-hooks' to maintain the spiritual glow of a life that is decisive in its commitment to the will of God.

2   THE SILENCE OF DISDAINFULNESS IN CONTEMPT FOR THE ENEMIES OF GOD

The Lord did not accuse His enemies of injustice. He just did not reply to their slander or answer the false witnesses. To argue with those who were bent on His death would have been futile. The result would only have been greater fury and further sin. 'Who, when He was reviled, reviled not again; when He suffered, He threatened not; but committed Himself to Him that judgeth righteously.' (I Peter 2:23)

The best reply to false accusation is silence, yet how quick we are to rise up in self-defence. How sensitive we are to criticism, and how eager to prove ourselves right! You will recall David's attitude when harassed by

Saul, his lifelong enemy. On at least two occasions he had a wonderful opportunity to deal with him finally and be rid of him, but he refused. Even when his right-hand man, Abishai, offered to do it for him, he refused to permit it, replying, 'As the Lord liveth, the Lord shall smite him; or his day shall come to die; or he shall descend into battle, and perish. The Lord forbid that I should stretch forth mine hand against the Lord's anointed (I Samuel 26:10-11). David would neither defend himself, nor would he allow anyone else to do it for him.

There is a story in Amy Carmichael's book, GOLD BY MOONLIGHT, of a minister who was slanderously accused, and for many years suffered from malicious gossip. One day his daughter was asked by her Sunday school teacher how her father had reacted to all that had been said against him, and the girl replied, 'This experience has made it impossible for my father to speak a word unkindly against anyone.'

Has the Lord taught you that lesson? It is a costly one, for the flesh revolts against it, and cries out for recognition and vindication. It shrinks from being put in a bad light in the eyes of others, but what a blessed release when we commit ourselves to Him that judges righteously, and allow Him to deal with the situation. That does not necessarily mean that in this life we will be proved right, but it does mean the assent of the flesh to the principle of death, and therefore the anointing of the life with the power of the Holy Spirit, and that is all that matters.

How many a Christian has lost that anointing for the sake of trying to defend himself. We need to constantly pray that the Lord will teach us when silence is golden.

3   THE SILENCE OF DEFENCELESSNESS IN CONSENT TO THE JUDGMENT OF GOD

There is a meaning in His silence deeper than anything we have yet considered. Nothing can be said to excuse human guilt, therefore He who bore its full weight stood speechless before the judge. 'He was led as a lamb to the slaughter.' Do you see how completely He is identified with us? Read Isaiah 53:6. Not only are we compared with sheep, but so is He.

I can understand that we should be likened to sheep and He to the shepherd, but that He too should be a sheep ... who but God would dare make that comparison?

Yet it is the theme of Scripture. 'Behold the Lamb of God, that beareth away the sin of the world' (John 1:29). He became what we were in order that we might become what He is (2 Corinthians 5:21).

Here is the deepest meaning of His silence. The Law had spoken, 'what things soever the law saith, it saith to them who are under the law: that every mouth may be stopped, and all the world may become guilty before God' (Romans 3:19). A silent world, condemned and with no argument to plead and no excuse to make, silently awaits the sentence of its doom. But, praise God, in place of a silent world stands a silent Jesus, led as a lamb to the slaughter and dumb before the shearers. There He stands in your place and mine, defenceless, as He consents to bear the judgment due to us.

The silence of Jesus! That is a lonely road along which none of us can travel. He trod the winepress alone. Yet there is something we can do, indeed we must do, if we are to enter into the significance of this truth.

Have you ever stood in the presence of the Lord with bowed head and heart, silent and without excuse or argument, with no defence or complaint, and said, 'Lord, I am wrong and You are right; I consent to Your judgment, for I am absolutely defenceless. I look alone to Jesus and His righteousness.' It is only at such a moment that the power of the Holy Spirit is released in your life.

Have you confessed resentment to the Lord? The times when others may have spoken against you and about you and you have resented it, then you have forfeited the anointing of His Holy Spirit. How much the Lord has lost of your life at that time! Confess your resentment in the presence of the One who bore so much hatred in silence.

Have you finally laid down the sword of your rebellion against the Lord? Confess your hesitating, half-hearted commitment to the will of God, and gladly abandon yourself to Him with the same measure of love in which the Lord Jesus abandoned His life in order to win yours.

❦ HERMON HOEKSEMA

Herman Hoeksema was professor of Dogmatics and New Testament Exegesis in the Protestant Reformed Seminary at Grand Rapids, Michigan, USA. He was also the author of such well known books on the passion and death of our Lord as THE ROYAL SUFFERER, REJECTED OF MEN, THE POWER OF THE CROSS and THE AMAZING CROSS. In the following sermon, taken from his book MAN OF SORROWS, Hoeksema, always provocative, does not fail to provide a new insight into the redemptive love of God, revealed in the substitutionary sufferings of the MAN OF SORROWS of Isaiah 53, by Whose stripes we are healed.

Chapter seven

WITH THE RICH IN HIS DEATH

'HE WAS TAKEN FROM PRISON AND FROM JUDGMENT: AND WHO SHALL DECLARE HIS
GENERATION? FOR HE WAS CUT OFF OUT OF THE LAND OF THE LIVING: FOR THE
TRANSGRESSION OF MY PEOPLE WAS HE STRICKEN.' — ISAIAH 53:8

THE SUFFERING SERVANT OF THE LORD HAD REACHED THE END
OF HIS EARTHLY LIFE.

Whatever may be the correct translation of verse 8 of Chapter 53 of
Isaiah's prophecy, this is certain: He was taken away from the land of the
living.

It is not easy to translate that eighth verse, and we shall not enter into
detail concerning it here because we wish to call special attention to
verse nine. The Authorised Version translates verse eight as follows: 'HE
WAS TAKEN FROM PRISON AND FROM JUDGMENT: AND WHO SHALL DECLARE HIS
GENERATION? FOR HE WAS CUT OFF OUT OF THE LAND OF THE LIVING: FOR THE
TRANSGRESSION OF MY PEOPLE WAS HE STRICKEN.' The Revised Version has a
considerably different translation: 'By oppression and judgment he was
taken away: and as for his generation, who among them considered that
he was cut off out of the land of the living for the transgression of my

people to whom the stroke was due?' We prefer the rendering: 'He had been taken away from prison and from judgment: and as for his generation, no one considered that he was snatched away out of the land of the living for the wickedness of his people, whose punishment fell upon him.'

But whatever may be the proper translation of this verse, this much is certain: it emphasises the end of the Suffering Servant of Jehovah as far as His earthly life was concerned. He was snatched away out of the land of the living.

It is finished, as the Lord Himself declared from the cross. The plague had been upon Him. He had been stricken with the punishment of His people. Not until He had perfectly borne the iniquities of those whom the Father had given Him, and had voluntarily sacrificed Himself in the love of God for the sins of His people, could he be snatched away. But now His earthly work was finished, and He was taken away from the land of the living.

Since He had finished all at that moment when He gave up the ghost, He could suffer shame and contempt no more. Already the Servant of the Lord is justified before God. Hence we read in verse nine: 'And he made his grave with the wicked, and with the rich in his death; because he had done no violence, neither was any conceit in his mouth.'

We cannot agree with the interpretation that is implied in the Revised Version: 'And they made his grave with the wicked, and with the rich man in his death; although he had done no violence, neither was any deceit in his mouth.' This interpretation presupposes that the rich man who is mentioned in this verse is the same as the wicked who are referred to in the first part of this text. The meaning then is that His grave was indeed assigned with the wicked, and that the enemies also succeeded in giving Him in His death a place among the ungodly. This is erroneous. In the first place, it is an error to identify the rich man in the text with the wicked. In the second place, it is then necessary to introduce the second part of the text by the conjunction 'although,' which is impossible according to the Hebrew original. And in the third place, this is in conflict with the history of Jesus' burial according to the gospel narratives. Therefore we prefer to circumscribe the meaning of this text in this way: 'Although the enemies indeed assigned his grave with the wicked, yet he was given an honourable burial with the rich, and that too, because he had done no violence, neither was any deceit found in his mouth.'

JESUS WAS BURIED.

He died the physical death, and His spirit separated from His earthly frame, as with dying lips He Himself announced from the cross in His last prayer: 'Father, into thy hands do I commend my spirit.' And it was necessary that He too should die the physical death, the death of the body. He might not simply suffer the agonies of death on the cross, in order then to be revived or glorified in the sight of the enemies, and ascend up to heaven. He must bear the wrath of God to the end. Physical death is God's declaration that the sinner has absolutely forfeited every right to his existence in the world. And this sentence was executed upon Christ also. God takes away His entire earthly house. His very name perishes. His body, too, collapses. And He gives up the ghost. Upon Him also the sentence is pronounced that He is unworthy to exist on earth. Death belongs to the wages of sin, also physical death. It is the expression of the wrath of God, the revelation of His justice against the sinner. Only, in the case of the Suffering Servant of the Lord, He made also of physical death an act, an act of love to God. He lays down His life willingly, even at the moment when God takes it away. His spirit He commends to the Father; His body He delivers over into the place of corruption. His name and position He freely offers up to the righteousness of God. And in delivering up His soul unto death He confesses that God is just when He judges that the sinner must be utterly destroyed from the earth. Christ therefore willingly performed the act of dying.

AND SO HE DESCENDED INTO THE GRAVE, THE PLACE OF PHYSICAL CORRUPTION.

In Question and Answer 41 the Heidelberg Catechism explains that

He was buried in order to prove that He was really dead. However, even apart from the fact that a man is not buried to prove that he is dead, such proof on the part of Christ was hardly necessary. That He had died before He was taken down from the cross was evident in His own outcry, commending His spirit to the Father. Besides, it is also evident from the spear-thrust in His side by one of the soldiers while He was still hanging on the cross. We read in John 19:31; 'The Jews therefore, because it was the preparation, that the bodies should not remain upon the cross on the sabbath day, (for that sabbath day was a high day), besought Pilate that their legs might be broken, and that they might be taken away. Then came the soldiers,, and brake the legs of the first, and of the other which was crucified with him. But when they came to Jesus, and saw that He was dead already, they brake not His legs: But one of the soldiers with a spear pierced His side, and forthwith came there out blood and water.' And the apostle John explains this incident as a fulfilment of scripture: 'A bone of Him shall not be broken. And again another scripture saith, They shall look on Him whom they pierced.' But Christ must die to the very end. He too must be buried. And although, according to scripture, He did not see corruption, He must enter the place of corruption nevertheless. He must deliver His body to the humiliation of the grave, to the place where the sinner returns to the dust. In perfect obedience to the Father He enters into Hades, and commits His body to the grave. And this too was a voluntary act on the part of the Suffering Servant of Jehovah. Just as He entered into the womb of the virgin, to assume the likeness of sinful flesh, so He obediently submitted to the sentence of God, 'Dust thou art, and to dust thou shalt return.' That He could do so, and that even His entering into the grave was a voluntary act of His own, may be explained from the fact that He was the Son of God, and the Person of the Son was never separated from His human nature, even in His death and in the grave.

SO HE ACCOMPLISHED ALL OF DEATH, AND FULFILLED ALL RIGHTEOUSNESS.

Now although the Jews had assigned His grave with the wicked, He nevertheless was with the rich in His death. There is, therefore, a significant symbolism in the burial of Jesus.

In the grave we see OUR aspect of temporal death. Temporal death is the final earthly separation of spirit and body in man. It has, therefore, two aspects: an aspect that refers to the earthly and material, and an aspect that refers to the spiritual and eternal side of man's existence. The grave is our aspect, that which we see of temporal death. We keep the dead body, and the spirit proceeds to God. Again, temporal death is twofold, as we know from Holy Writ. For the ungodly it is a passage into eternal desolation. This is true immediately after death of the soul, or spirit. We read of the rich man in the parable: 'The rich man also died and was buried; And in hell he lifted up his eyes, being in torments, and seeth Abraham afar off, and Lazarus in his bosom. And he cried and said, Father Abraham, have mercy on me, and send Lazarus, that he may dip the tip of his finger in water, and cool my tongue; for I am tormented in this flame' (Luke 16:22-24). And as to the body of the ungodly, it is simply waiting in the grave for its eternal desolation, beginning in the morning of the resurrection. For thus we read in John 5:28,29: 'Marvel not at this: for the hour is coming in the which all that are in the graves shall hear his voice. And shall come forth; they that have done good, unto the resurrection of life; and they that have done evil, unto the resurrection of damnation.' But for the godly, in distinction from the wicked, physical death is a passage into everlasting glory. That this is true is evident from what the Lord said to the one malefactor who was crucified with Him: 'Today thou shalt be with me in paradise.' And in 2 Corinthians 5:1 we read: 'For we know that if our earthly house of this tabernacle were dissolved, we have a building of God, an house not made with hands, eternal in the heavens.' The soul of the godly, therefore, immediately passes on to heavenly glory. And as to his body, it is simply sown in the earth, that presently it may appear in the glory of the resurrection: 'It is sown in corruption; it is raised in incorruption: It is sown in dishonour; it is raised in glory: it is sown in weakness; it is raised in power: it is sown a natural body; it is raised a spiritual body' (I Corinthians 15:42-44). For this reason we said that in the burial and in the grave there is a significant symbolism.

In several places of scripture we find that the wicked are not entitled to an honourable burial together with the righteous. But in scripture the separation of the righteous and the wicked in burial is emphasised more than once. When carnal Israel rebels against Jehovah in the desert, the Lord threatens through Moses and Aaron: 'Your carcases shall fall in this wilderness' (Numbers 14:29; Hebrews 3:17). Isaiah prophesises of wicked Babylon: 'But thou art cast out of thy grave like an abominable branch, and as the raiment of those that are slain, thrust through with the sword, that go down to the stones of the pit; as a carcase trodden under feet. Thou shalt not be joined with them in burial' (Isaiah 14:19,20). And of the carnal and ungodly children of Judah Jeremiah prophesies: 'And the carcases of this people shall be meat for the fowls of the heaven, and for the beasts of the earth; and none shall fray them away' (Jeremiah 7:33). And of king Jehoiakim we read: 'They shall not lament for him, saying, Ah my brother! or, Ah sister! they shall not lament for him, saying, Ah Lord! or, Ah his glory! He shall be buried with the burial of an ass, drawn and cast forth beyond the gates of Jerusalem' (Jeremiah 22:19). And again, of the wicked children of Judah we read: 'I will even give them into the hand of their enemies, and into the hand of them that seek their life: and their dead bodies shall be for meat unto the fowls of heaven, and to the beasts of the earth' (Jeremiah 34:20). On the other hand, it is a lamentable thing when the righteous and the saints of God suffer the same lot with the wicked, and are not honourably buried. About this the psalmist complains in Psalm 79:1,2: 'O God, the heathen are come into thine inheritance; thy holy temple have they defiled; they have laid Jerusalem on heaps. The dead bodies of thy servants have they given to be meat unto the fowls of the heaven, the flesh of thy saints unto the beasts of the earth.' In the symbolism of the grave, therefore, it is made plain that although the righteous and the wicked live promiscuously on the earth in this present life, in physical and temporal death they separate forever. For the soul of the righteous passes into glory, that of the wicked into desolation. And the body of the righteous awaits in the grave the morning of the glorious resurrection, that of the wicked the morning of the resurrection of damnation.

Now according to the passage of Isaiah we are discussing at present, the enemies of the Lord had assigned His grave with the wicked. During His life they had reckoned Him with the transgressors. As a transgressor they had captured Him in Gethsemane, had led Him to the Sanhedrin and to Pilate. They had accused Him and condemned Him to death. He had been killed as the worst malefactor, between two murderers, as one that is accursed of God. And the intention of the hostile Jews was that He also should be buried as such. They assigned His grave with the wicked. That is the meaning of the text. And this is evident also from the history recorded in the gospel narratives. For according to John 19:31, the Jews came to Pilate and besought him that the legs of all three malefactors might be broken, in order that the bodies might not remain on the cross on the sabbath day. And if this had been done, the bodies would simply have been put into the ground in the neighbourhood of the cross without any formal or honourable burial. They would have done this also to the body of Jesus. Then He would not have been buried at all, but simply, perhaps with His cross, been put under the ground. And the Jews would have expressed by this act that Jesus had passed on into eternal desolation, accursed of God, forever separated from the righteous, and that also His body should not share the resurrection of the just. When they assigned His grave with the wicked, they designated that His proper place was with the eternally damned.

BUT IN THIS THE JEWS DID NOT SUCCEED.

According to the text, He was with the rich in His death. And although being rich is not a proper antithesis to being wicked, neither does it stand in direct contrast to being righteous. Besides, the rich usually see that their loved ones are buried honourably. This, moreover, is the only interpretation of the text in Isaiah that is possible in the light of the gospel narratives concerning Jesus' burial. The rich man was Joseph of Arimathea, who together with Nicodemus was a disciple of Jesus, though secretly for fear of the Jews. And he waited for the kingdom of God (Matthew 27:57; Mark 15:43; Luke 23:50,51; John 19:38). He approached

Pilate and begged for the body of Jesus. He evidently feared the worst, and understood that the hostile Jews would assign His grave with the wicked. And this he was anxious to prevent. Pilate apparently was at first reluctant to give his consent. But when he marvelled once more at Jesus because he heard from the centurion that He had already died, he gave the body to Joseph (Mark 15:44,45). Thus Jesus received a very honourable burial. For the body was wrapped in fine linen, together with spices, a mixture of myrrh and aloes, about an hundred pound weight, which Nicodemus had brought. And Jesus' body was laid in a new rock-hewn sepulchre, wherein never man was yet laid (John 19:39-41). And a heavy stone was rolled in front of the sepulchre.

Thus, although the Jews had assigned His grave with the wicked, He was nevertheless with the rich in His death.

In this burial of the righteous which was given to Jesus God already showed that His Suffering Servant was justified.

O, it is true, His glorious resurrection was the special proof that God justified Him, and that we are justified with Him. For He 'was delivered for our offences, and was raised again for our justification.' Nevertheless, His burial also was the beginning of His glorification, and therefore of His justification. That is why the reason for this honourable burial is expressed in the last part of Isaiah 53:9, 'because he had done no violence, neither was any deceit in his mouth.'

Personally Christ was the Sinless One. The sin of the race in Adam could not be imputed to Him. He had no original guilt, for personally He was the Son of God. Nor did He have original defilement and corruption, for the chain of corruption was broken in His case by the conception of the Holy Spirit. Nor did He personally have any actual sin. Always He was motivated by the love of God, and walked in perfect obedience even in the midst of a wicked world. He did no wrong. An evil word never proceeded out of His mouth. He always did the will of the Father. Moreover, even when He bore the sins of His people, and God laid on Him the iniquity of us all, He committed no sin whatsoever. On the contrary, He was always obedient. Every moment of His life in the world the Father in heaven could say to Him: 'This is my beloved Son, in whom I am well pleased.' Even when He was counted with the transgressors, He nevertheless was the Sinless One. Even then He did no injustice, nor was any deceit ever found in His mouth.

Therefore, now that all was finished and the Lamb of God had completely taken away the sin of the world, it was the Father's will that in His burial He should be reckoned with the transgressors no more, but counted with the righteous. His spirit was already with the Father in heavenly glory, and His body waited in the sepulchre of Joseph of Arimathea for the morning of the glorious resurrection. Hence, although His enemies assigned His grave with the wicked, the Lord so directed the affairs of men that He received a place with the rich in His death.

THE BURIAL OF JESUS, THEREFORE, WAS THE BEGINNING OF HIS JUSTIFICATION.

The burial of Jesus is our comfort. For it teaches us what the Lord God judges about the grave of the righteous. When they die, they shall go with Him into paradise, while their body rests in the grave.

And presently the corruptible body shall put on incorruption, and the mortal body shall put on immortality. And death shall be swallowed up in victory.

With their eye on the place of corruption in the light of the burial of the Suffering Servant of the Lord, the people of God may well shout: 'O death, where is thy sting? O grave, where is thy victory? The sting of death is sin; and the strength of sin is the law. But thanks be to God which giveth us the victory through our Lord Jesus Christ.'

❦ THOMAS MANTON

Thomas Manton was born in Somerset in 1620. He entered the University of Oxford in 1635, and graduated with a Bachelor of Arts in 1639. The following year he was ordained by Bishop Hall, at the age of nineteen, and thus began his ministry. His first appointment was in Stoke Newington, Middlesex, where he served for seven years. He soon became very popular and frequently preached before the members of Parliament, taking part in public events such as the Westminster Assembly, and the publication of the Westminster Confession.

In 1656 he was called to succeed Obadiah Sedgwick as Rector of St. Paul's, Covent Garden, London. His ministry attracted crowds of nobility and Archbishop Ussher called him 'one of the best preachers in England.' As such he served as a chaplain to the Lord Protector, Oliver Cromwell, and was an acknowledged leader of the Presbyterians.

Manton died in 1677, leaving behind him a rich legacy of practical biblical ministry. William Bates, when preaching at his funeral, said of him that he was a man 'endowed with an extraordinary knowledge in the scriptures and this enabled him to exercise a sustained ministry of verse by verse preaching without losing the interest of his congregation.'

This sermon, taken from Vol. 3 of THE WORKS OF THOMAS MANTON, represents Puritan preaching at its very best.

Chapter eight

CHRIST - THE GREAT EXAMPLE

<small>AND HE MADE HIS GRAVE WITH THE WICKED, AND WITH THE RICH IN HIS DEATH;
BECAUSE HE HAD DONE NO VIOLENCE, NEITHER WAS ANY DECEIT IN HIS MOUTH.
- ISAIAH 53:9</small>

THE PROPHET GOETH ON WITH THE ACCOUNT OF CHRIST'S SUFFERINGS, AND SHOWETH THAT HE SHOULD AT LENGTH BE humbled to the grave, and brought thither in a most ignominious manner. Yet, however, there was no cause why the Jews should stumble at it, and dash the foot of their faith against this rock, for God had made provision ample enough against this offence and scandal. Even his grave, that seemed to obscure his glory, did in some measure illustrate it: 'He made his grave with the wicked, and with the rich in his death, because he had done no violence, neither was any deceit in his mouth.'

Here are in this verse, as in many of the former, two parts considerable:-

1   The Jews' scandal: HE MADE HIS GRAVE WITH THE WICKED

2   The prophet's defence, which you have –
-   By the circumstances which made for the glory of Christ: AND WITH THE
    RICH IN HIS DEATH.
-   By asserting his innocency-
    In respect of open and gross sins: HE HATH DONE NO VIOLENCE.

    In respect of secret and hidden sins: NEITHER WAS ANY DECEIT FOUND IN HIS
MOUTH. All these parts will more plainly appear in the explication. There
are no verses have been so severally expounded as this and the former. I
should perplex your thoughts too much to give you the differences. Some
distinct senses there are: I shall only give you what I conceive to be the
positive and plain sense, by going over the phrases.

AND HE MADE.

    There may be a question to whom this HE must be referred, for the
number being so often changed, we can have no relief from the context.
There are three persons spoken of in the chapter: God the Father, God
the Son, and the Jews. If this HE be applied to God the Father, then the
sense is, he disposed and ordered it so by his providence that his grave
should be appointed among the wicked; and so it points at the divine
decrees, which implied that Christ should be executed as an offender,
and be buried in an ignominious manner, as other offenders are, for aught
could be discerned at first. This suiteth with the Seventy, who bring in
God the Father speaking this clause, though they read the sentence a
little otherwise that we do: 'I will give the wicked for his grave.' Or it may
be referred to God the Son, - his patience, who submitted so, as it seemed
to hold forth nothing but as if he were to have had the burial of an
ordinary malefactor, he submitting to it till a further declaration of God's
pleasure; a man could have guessed nothing else. Or, HE MADE, may be
referred to the people of the Jews; they did as much as in them lay that
Christ should have the burial of a wicked man: 'He made,' that is, by their
ordination. You may take either or all very commodiously. It followeth,
'and with the rich in his death.' There is a great deal ado about what is

meant by rich. Some understand the term, as Calvin, equivalent with the wicked; because riches puff up men's minds and dispose them to injury and violence. Junius understands Pilate; others have different apprehensions of the place. I shall take liberty to recede from them; for by this phrase, 'the rich in his death,' I understand Joseph of Armiathea; and the meaning I conceive thus, that though at his crucifixion his grave was intended to be with ordinary malefactors,, yet God ordered it so that he should be honourably interred by a rich person, Joseph of Arimathea: 'With the rich in his death,' that is, after his death. And my reasons for this interpretation are two:-

1. Because the word for rich, AASIR, in the Hebrew, is in the singular number, and so noteth some eminent rich man that had to do about the grave and sepulchre of Christ; and that was Joseph of Arimathea.

2. Because the evangelist Matthew seemeth, as with a finger, to point to this place when he saith, Matthew 27:57-58, 'When the even was come, there came a rich man of Arimathea, named Joseph, who also himself was Jesus' disciple. He went to Pilate, and begged the body of Jesus.' And besides, the place is most sweetly and without wresting opened. And, indeed, the following words yield us a twofold reason:-

i) Because God would right his innocency in the midst of calumnies and reproaches. God would not have an innocent buried among malefactors; and, therefore, by the care of Joseph and Nicodemus, he would have it testified to the world that there were some thought him innocent and worthy of an honourable burial.

ii) It may well be to show the suitableness of it. He would have a new kind of man laid in a new grave, in which no man was ever laid. It could be said of no man but Christ that no iniquity and guile was found in him; and therefore he was put in a sepulchre in which no man was laid. For now God began to honour Christ because he had done no violence. In Peter, it is, 'Who did no sin;' for indeed the word must be taken so generally. It is meant, no gross fact could be charged upon him; neither was there any deceit in his mouth; that is, he was guilty of no secret evil: for no guile in the mouth argueth there was none in the heart – there being a swift intercourse between the heart and the tongue: James 3:2, 'If any man offend not in word, the same is perfect man, able to bridle the whole body.'

Thus for the phrases. The sum of all is this, that though the Messiah was taken away by a shameful death, and therefore likely to be looked upon as an eminent instance of divine wrath and vengeance, yet the Lord provided for his glory in the midst of this ignominy, by procuring such a sepulchre and burial for him as might set out not only his innocency but his honour; for he indeed was without fault and blame. There is not much to be observed out of this verse, yet that which is, is very comfortable, and therefore in the general take these notes.

1   There is a sweet harmony and accord between the Old and New Testament; they agree in the least things. Isaiah saith, 'He made his grave with the rich;' and Matthew saith, 'a rich man of Arimathea came and begged his body.' So in other things you may observe there is an agreement in those things which a man would judge to be of least consequence.

2   That every passage of Christ's life is considerable; as this concerning the account of his burial. A man would have thought it had not been so worthy of observation, and yet the prophet speaketh of it as an eminent circumstance, and you shall see much use may be made of it by and by. So, for Christ's name, Matthew 1:23, 'They shall call his name Emmanuel, which, being interpreted, is, God with us.' So the offering for him a pair of turtle-doves and two young pigeons. Man would easily overlook these things, yet the Holy Ghost thought them worthy the noting. Oh, study Christ's life more; there is no waste passage in it. But what benefit is there in the text? I shall not here give you doctrines, as I did from the other verses, but direct you, for your comfort, to look upon Christ under a threefold notion, viz., as our surety, as a pattern of providence, and as a great example.

I   As a surety; so there are two clauses that afford comfort to
believers:-

i) That 'he made his grave with the wicked, and with the rich in his
death.' That expression, 'He made his grave with the wicked,' holdeth
forth the payment of the debt, and full evidence of his satisfaction.
Your surety suffered in your stead. 'Cursed is every one that continueth
not in all things which are written in the book of the law to do them.'
And the Lord Christ was accursed to redeem us from the curse of law.
But I shall chiefly take notice of this circumstance, 'And with the rich
in his death.' After Christ had once died, God began to honour him:
full satisfaction being made to God, and the reproach and shame due
to sins taken away; after death he had an honourable interment. Of all
people, the Jews did most look to burials. It was a great threatening
that they should die unburied: Proverbs 30:17, 'The eye that mocketh
at his father, the ravens of the valley shall pick it out, and the young
eagles shall eat it;' alluding to the shameful death and burial of the
disobedient son.' And again, Psalm 79:3, There should be 'none to
bury him.' And Jeremiah 22:19, 'He shall be buried with the burial of
an ass, drawn and cast forth beyond the gates of Jerusalem.' But now
Christ had not only a decent but an honourable burial. Well, then,
Christians, here is encouragement for your faith. Christ was honoured
as soon as he died: the work is ended – the last act of his humiliation
was the first step to his exaltation, and there began his triumph and
glory. Joseph and Nicodemus, two of his devout followers, they
celebrate his funeral, and bury him with such solemnities as are due
to persons of the greatest honour. Well, then, conclude in faith, that
by Christ's death, shame, and sufferings, sin is done away. Christians
were wont to solemnise their funerals with psalms of thanksgiving.
You may remember Christ's funeral with rejoicing and giving of thanks:
there you have the first intimation that the work was finished, sins
were satisfied for, shame and reproach began to vanish. O you
redeemed of the Lord, go forth and rejoice. God beginneth to take off
the ignominy of Christ's death, and thereby your ignominy and your
shame. So that now, 'In him we have boldness and access with

confidence by the faith of him,' Ephesians 3:12; that is, you may freely
have communion and social commerce with God, your shame being
gone; God hath branded sin with shame. Adam hid himself; the
captains and great men called to the mountains to cover them from
the wrath of the Lamb, they could not endure the sight of God. Guilt
maketh a fallen countenance, and causeth a shyness of God. Now you
may lift up your heads, your shame is taken away.

ii) From that clause, 'Because he had done no violence, neither was any
deceit in his mouth.' Your surety was a pure person – he had no guilt
of his own to satisfy for, and so it yieldeth not only an encouragement
to faith, but an endearment of love to Christ. All these sufferings were
for you, there is nothing that can argue a need for himself to do it.
The scriptures everywhere urge and testify this: I John 3:5, 'And ye
know that he was manifested to take away our sins, and in him is no
sin.' All his sufferings were for some cause: there was nothing to
occasion them in himself, it must therefore be for our sins: I Peter
3:18, 'For Christ hath also once suffered for sin, the just for the
unjust, that he might bring us to God.' It was for sins he suffered, and
therefore certainly for ours, for he had none of his own. Urge it then
upon your hearts, both as an encouragement to faith and an
endearment to love. It was a pure Christ that suffered, and therefore
certainly for such an impure wretch as I am – the just for the unjust.
Reason thus: Surely God is just; Christ undergoing so great sufferings,
and yet possessed of great purity, certainly died for great sinners.

2 As a pattern of providence. God meant to copy out all dispensations
in the life of Christ. Learn then:-

i) That we must not always look upon the face of providence and eye
present appearances, 'He made his grave with the wicked, and
with the rich in his death.' A man would have thought that Christ
should have had an ignominious burial, and that none would have
contributed to his glory; but the rich man begged his body from the
cross, and God turns his grave into his glory. Oh, do not look to

present appearance; you know not what a mercy may be couched under the frowns of providence. John 2:7, Christ calleth for waterpots when he meant to give them wine; and John 11:6, when he meant to restore Lazarus from the dead by a miracle, he would not vouchsafe to go and see him; he abode still two days in the same place. When God designed to honour Christ with a funeral, he meant to order it so that the Jews looked for nothing else but the burial of an ass. Thus God many times seems to hide himself, and when we seek for him, he is not to be found: Ecclesiastes 11:4, 'He that observeth the wind shall not sow, and he that regardeth the clouds shall not reap.' If you look always upon the face of outward things, the heart will be discouraged with the louring of Providence.

ii) Learn what reason you have to wait upon God when things are at the worst. There was no appearance for Christ till things came to the worst. Joseph begged his body when dead upon the cross: 'He was with the rich in his death;' Job 13:15, 'Though he slay me, yet will I trust in him.' God can of a sudden turn things, and disappoint the devices and counsels of wicked men, even when they think all is sure. Therefore wait upon God, and see what event he will give to things. When the Jews thought every one would be ashamed of Christ, up start Joseph and Nicodemus, and boldly begged his body. There was death first before God would do him honour.

iii) Look upon him as the great example; so there is benefit in the last clause: 'For he had done no violence, neither was there deceit in his mouth.' This is your pattern: I Peter 2:21-22, 'Because Christ also suffered for us, leaving us an example that we should follow his steps, who did no sin, neither was guile found in his mouth.' Oh that we could write after this fair copy that Christ hath set us, that we might be 'holy as he was holy in all manner of conversation,' I Peter 1:15, in every turning of our lives. I would not that you should lose the benefit of this instruction for want of making it particular. I shall set home this pattern by the two words of the text, VIOLENCE and DECEIT. None of this was found in Christ.

1 VIOLENCE. Take heed of that. There is violence in the spirit, manifested
by wrath, revenge, boisterousness of passion, affection. Oh, what an
unbecoming thing it is for men to deliver themselves over to the sway
of their own passions! James 1:20, 'The wrath of man worketh not the
righteousness of God.' The meaning is, such a heart is not fit to serve
God; it will not reach righteousness. God must have always service
proportionate. God, that is a spirit, must be served in spirit and in
truth; the God of peace with peace, with a peaceable, calm spirit: I
Timothy 2:8, 'Lifting up holy hands without wrath and doubting.' Then
there is violence in the tongue, showed in bitterness, reviling,
reproaches. This was far from Christ; he did no violence. This becometh
the sons of the world rather than the sons of God. Surely such wolfish
dispositions do ill become them that are related to the Lamb, the
Lamb slain for the sins of the world. Where is your warrant for this in
the life of Christ? Galatians 5:15, 'If ye bite and devour one another,
take heed ye be not consumed one of another.' You learn it of the wolf
or the old dragon, not of the Lamb. The apostle useth such a word as
implieth such bitterness as is brutish. Then in practice, by opression,
invading of another's right and property. There was no such thing in
Christ. He would not intrench upon the magistrate's office: John 8:11,
'Neither do I condemn thee; go and sin no more.' Not in respect of
guilt, for he saith, 'Sin no more.' But the meaning is, he would not
meddle with her punishment; it was none of his office, and therefore
he would not in the least manner encroach upon another's right. Learn
of Christ, who did no violence.

2 There was no DECEIT found in his mouth. Take heed also of that. Be
like Christ. It is said of Nathanael, John 1:47, 'Behold an Israelite
indeed, in whom there is no guile.' Why an Israelite indeed? Because,
like old Israel, like old Jacob; for it is said of him, Genesis 25:27,
'Jacob was a plain man, and dwelt in tents.' So here; we are Christians
indeed when without guile, when we are like Christ, for no deceit was
found in him. There is deceit in heart, which the scripture calleth
guile of spirit: Psalm 32:2, 'Blessed is the man unto whom the Lord
imputeth not iniquity, and in whose spirit there is no guile.' Take heed

of this deceitful heart. We must take heed we drive not on a self-design in all our respects to God and men; and when we pretend to zeal in worship, that it is not to serve ourselves of it. Revelation 14:5, it is said of the Lamb's followers, that 'in their mouth was found no guile;' they are without fault before the throne of God, Hebrews 4:12. Wait upon the word, for that is 'a divider between soul and spirit, and of the joints and marrow, and is a discerner of the thoughts and the intention of the heart;' that is, between fairness of pretences, and vileness of affection and baseness of intents. And there is deceit in the mouth when men dissemble for advantage. You did not learn this of Jesus Christ. As Doeg glavered upon David, to tell Saul of it: Psalm 120:3, 'What shall be done unto thee, thou false tongue?' Though he told the truth, yet he flattered with David, that he might observe his carriage, and relate it to Saul: Psalm 52:4, 'Thou lovest all devouring words, O thou deceitful tongue.' Then for practice, many give out specious pretences, as if they were what indeed they are not. Be what you would be accounted to be. It is hypocrisy that overacts to the world. We know counterfeit gold because it looketh so yellow: 2 Samuel 15:6, Absalom stole the hearts of the men of Israel by flattery, and fair but false pretences. But we should eye our pattern. That is true religion, to imitate Him whom we worship.

❧ Ian MacPherson

I an MacPherson served for fifty-three years as a minister of the Apostolic Church, including six years as the Principal of the Apostolic Bible College in Penygroes, South Wales. He was also a former editor of the magazine, PROPHETIC WITNESS.

He was the author of several books of sermons including a survey of Christian doctrine, entitled THE FAITH ONCE DELIVERED. In a former work THE BURDEN OF THE LORD, he maintains that 'preaching is not the bare utterance of words, however skilfully woven on the loom of literacy or oratorical art; it is infinitely more – the communication of the Word.'

This sermon is taken from GOD'S MIDDLEMAN which was first published in 1965.

Chapter nine

THE PROGENY OF JESUS

'...He shall see his seed...' – Isaiah 53:10

JESUS FOUNDED NO FAMILY. IN THIS HE DIFFERED FROM MOST OF THE GREAT MORAL TEACHERS OF MANKIND. THEY WERE nearly all married men. Confucius, the sage of ancient China, was wed at nineteen. Buddha had a wife and child, though he left both on the day of the baby's birth to begin the religious quest. Mohammed was a father, and permitted each of his male followers a maximum of four wives. But Jesus founded no family, produced no progeny, engendered no issue. In Biblical phrase, He did not 'see His seed.'

Now, among the old-world Hebrews, that was regarded, not just as it would be with ourselves, as a marital misfortune, but as something approaching a major personal tragedy. For the Jew set great store by his stock. He was immensely proud of his progeny. A man was famous as being the father of a large family. But Jesus – alone among the leaders of the religions of the race – was unmarried and therefore childless.

That is, of course, a matter of history. And yet here is the prophet, hundreds of years before the birth of Christ, predicting what appears to be the precise opposite.

Assuming that his words, although primarily applicable to the Jewish nation as a whole, or perhaps to some outstanding figure in it – Jeremiah, for instance – have nevertheless a proleptic reference to Jesus Christ, we find the prophet saying two things about our Lord which seem flatly contradictory and mutually exclusive. In one breath, he exclaims, 'Who shall declare His generation, for He was cut off out of the land of the living?' and in the next, 'He shall see His seed.'

What are we to make of this?

A clue is provided by the context. The setting helps us to perceive the sense. Note the conditioning clause which precedes the text: 'When Thou shalt make His soul an offering for sin, He shall see His seed.' Ah, that is it! The Offering is to produce the offspring. The sacrifice is to produce the sons. The cutting off is to produce the adding on.

And so it has! For although it is true, as a matter of history, that Jesus had no natural children, it is also true, as a matter of history, that ever since that distant day when they nailed Him to a Roman Cross, He has been begetting a numerous spiritual progeny. From that time forward He has been fathering a colossal family. And an hour is coming, so the Bible says, when out of every kindred and nation and tongue and people there is going to assemble a vast concourse all belonging to this holy household. And if you were to ask them how they came to be connected with the family of God, how it all started, where it all began, they would point back as if with one finger to the Cross, and they would cry: 'It was there that it happened. Calvary is our spiritual birthplace. The Offering has produced the offspring.'

'What a chorus, what a meeting,
With the family complete!'

As every preacher knows, there are, broadly speaking, two ways of tackling a text – the analytic and the synthetic. When, however, the text is tiny, as here, one is left with no alternative. One MUST treat it topically, for it won't divide. In casting about for some workman-like way of dealing with this scrap of scripture, I came upon an outline by an old Puritan, so masterly and so precisely pat to my purpose that I propose, modernizing it a little, to use it now. Seeing the author has been in his grave these three hundred years, I don't suppose he'll mind!

Take the points one by one.

BORN AND BROUGHT IN.

It goes without saying that there is only one way into a family – the way of birth. There is, of course, such a thing as adoption. It is impossible to institute legal proceedings whereby a child belonging by nature to one family can be officially incorporated into another. It is possible by such means for the child in question to enjoy the privilege of bearing the name of its new parents and of inheriting their wealth and property. I know all that – but I know this too: that none of these facts affects in the slightest the truth of the contention that there is only really one way into a family, the way of birth.

If Jesus is to see His seed, it can only be as people are BORN into His family. That is why in His dialogue with Nicodemus He was so insistent on the need for regeneration. 'Except a man be born again, he cannot see the kingdom of God.' (John 3:3). On the lips of the Omnipotent 'cannot' is a strong word. In this context it expresses the utter impossibility of anyone becoming a member of the family of God unless born and brought in.

And have we not all said at times with a sigh: 'If only I could have my life over again!' There is a sense, of course, in which we cannot. Neither the clock nor the calendar can ever be put back. Yet how often, like the rhymster, we wistfully exclaim:

'Oh, I wish there were some wonderful place
Called the Land of Beginning Again,
Where all our mistakes
And all our heart-aches
Could be dropped like a shabby old coat at the gate
And never put on again!'

Well, the almost incredible good news of the Gospel is that there is
such a place. There is a Land of Beginning Again. We CAN get rid of our
mistakes and heart-aches and leave the old life for ever behind. 'I wished,'
says Bunyan, describing the hour of his spiritual awakening, 'that I might
be a little child again.' Bunyan's wish came true. He actually became a
new creature in Christ Jesus. For him, old things passed away; all things
became new. Just as he received physical life from his father and mother
and thus became a member of their family, so he received spiritual life
from God through Christ and became a member of His family.

Some years ago I had occasion to call at the Belgian Embassy in
London. Entering the building, I was, without preface, accosted by a man,
a total stranger, who came up to me and said: 'Excuse me, sir, but has
anybody ever told you that you are uncommonly like the King of Spain!'
The King of Spain! My first reaction was to question the man's sanity; my
second was to feel sorry for the King of Spain! Anyhow, I pushed the
remark into a pigeon-hole in my mind and 'forgot' all about it. A month
or two later, however, I chanced to be in Scotland and, whilst there,
invited a cousin of mine to lunch in a Glasgow restaurant. Sitting next to
me at table, she remarked quite casually: 'I suppose you know that on
your mother's side of the family you originally hailed from Spain!' 'Spain!'
I said. 'I did not know that we had sprung from Spain!' 'Yes,' she replied,
'your family is definitely of Iberian descent.' 'Spain!' The word rang a
bell. It brought back to my recollection that curious observation in the
Belgian Embassy not long before. And presently I began to connect the
two things in my mind. I began to see that they belonged together. I was
like the King of Spain! My forbears had sprung from Spain! Between the
two facts there was evidently a living link. I was like the king because I
shared the life of the king!

Now that is a picture of what it means to be a Christian. It means to be
like the King because you have become a partaker of the life of the King.
'As many as received Him, to them gave He power to become the sons of
God, even to them that believe on His name.' (John 1:12).

There is the first of the old Puritans points – BORN AND BROUGHT IN!

EDUCATED AND BROUGHT UP.

How natural it is for children to want to be grown up! Always they are wishing their lives away, dreaming of adulthood and of the day when they will be children no longer. If you doubt that, ask a little girl of seven how old she is, and then watch her eyes sparkle as she replies: 'I'll be eight on my next birthday!' But then – if you dare! – ask a lady of thirty-seven how old she is, and see what happens! If she does not brusquely bid you mind your own business, she will probably tell you that she was thirty-five two years ago! Yes, it is perfectly natural for children to want to be grown-up; and the same laudable ambition ought to characterise the new-born members of the family of God.

But – DOES IT? Not always! In many churches today there is an appalling amount of spiritual infantilism. There are far too many Christian Peter Pans, people who have been brought in but have not been brought up.

Now, so far as God is concerned, there is no reason why this should be. He who provides for us a new nature likewise provides a new nurture; H e has made plans for the cultivation of the life which He bestows.

To come to the point, He has opened a school! 'If life is a playground,' wrote G. H. Morrison, 'I am a pessimist. If life is a school, then I desire to live.' Life IS a school and Christ is the teacher.

This emerges clearly from a figure Paul employs in his Epistle to the Galatians. The Authorised Version gives a wrong impression of the Apostle's meaning. 'The law' it says, 'was our schoolmaster to bring us to Christ.' That is not what Paul intended to convey.

"Schoolmaster,' comments Dr. Leslie F. Church, 'is a difficult word. In Greek it suggests the person who leads the child to the schoolhouse. The pedagogue (paidagogos), the word here used, was usually a family slave. The word literally signifies "the leader or keeper of childhood," and the idea was that the trusted servant should act as tutor to restrain and correct the child. Each day he should take his little charge to the school for instruction. When the child arrived at manhood the pedagogue was no longer required.'

You see the picture? The Law taking us by the hand to conduct us to the school of Christ! Are we in that school? Are we, from the lips of the supreme Master, learning how to live? Are we conning our lessons well and seeking to carry them out in everyday experience? Doing our homework?

Of Blaise Pascal, the pious and brilliant Frenchman, Professor Caillet beautifully wrote: 'At the school of his Master, and in His name, he stood at the door and knocked.' Samuel Rutherford expressed the hope that he might, as he phrased it, 'go in through the golden gates at last with my book open in my hand – still learning.' And John Wesley at eighty-six declared: 'I am still at school.' What an example such men set us! Michelangelo is said to have 'carried his satchel to the end of his days.' So did these great Christians, but their devotion was to an art higher than that of the famous painter – the art of life itself!

The spiritual maturity and infinite teachability of such saints is a rebuke to our dwarfed and stunted souls. You will remember the immortal passage of autobiography in which Paul testifies: 'When I was a child I spake as a child, I understood as a child, I thought as a child: but when I became a man I put away childish things.' Can we honestly claim that it is so with us?

I well remember that once, when we lived in London, our little daughter, then aged five, and I had occasion to wait for her mother at Piccadilly Circus. It was rush hour, and the traffic that day was even busier than usual. There was, however, in one tiny patch of pavement somewhat out of the stream of pedestrians and here, in the interval of waiting, the child soon fell to amusing herself, as children will, in so far as the limited space at her disposal would allow. Quite unconscious that she was being watched, she performed all sorts of curious antics – skipping with an imaginary rope, hopping about on one leg, pirouetting on the tips of her toes, and so on – much to the amusement of some of the passers-by. After completing one more than ordinarily violent physical contortion, she paused for a moment and looked up into my face, and there was a touch of challenge in her tone, as she said: 'You couldn't do that, Daddy? Could you?' Well of course I could have done it! There was nothing athletically impossible to me in the feat which she had just performed. I could have done it. But would I have done it? Not likely! You won't watch me pirouetting on the tips of my toes in Piccadilly Circus! You see, what was perfectly natural in a child of five would have been perfectly ridiculous in a man of thirty five!

Spiritually speaking, it is the same. If we have been members in Christ's family for years, it is high time we were grown up. We ought not to linger in the baby class, to loiter in the kindergarten. Nor ought we to display in our characters the pitiable spectacle of arrested spiritual development. By the grace of God, we ought to be making moral progress – overcoming temptations that once mastered us, handling adverse circumstances more successfully, deepening daily in our understanding of the great doctrines of the historic faith. 'Grow in grace,' enjoins Peter, 'and in the knowledge of our Lord and Saviour Jesus Christ' (2 Peter 3:18). 'Grow up into Him in all things,' says Paul, 'which is the Head, even Christ,' (Ephesians 4:15).

There is the old Puritan's second point: EDUCATED AND BROUGHT UP.

SUPPORTED AND BROUGHT THROUGH.

What a wonderful thing is the general providence of God! Just think! God has some two thousand nine hundred million mouths to feed – rather a large catering assignment – and He has been doing it daily for countless years and will go on doing it to the last syllable of recorded time.

I do not, of course, overlook the tragic fact to which the late Dr. Sangster called attention, that 'by scientific standards of nutrition one half of the world is hungry and a third of it is starving.' But that is not God's fault. It may seem pitifully naïve to sing:

'If we were all brothers, and loved one another,
The whole wide world could be fed,
On only two little fishes
And five loaves of bread.'

Yet there is more in the simple rhyme than appears on the surface. Said Keir Hardie, one of the pioneers of British Socialism: 'There is plenty in the world for all, if we would only help each other to it, or at least refrain from getting in each other's way: it is man's selfishness that limits it, and keeps it from starving mouths.' The failure, as any economist will tell you, is not really in production but in distribution. In other words, it's man's failure, not God's. How wonderful is divine providence!

Standing one day by the Thames Embankment in London, I saw a man leaning over the parapet. He was stretching his right arm out above the muddy waters of the river, the hand tightly closed as if clasping something. There was bread in that clenched palm, and the seagulls thereabouts knew that there was bread in it. Swooping swiftly down, the hungry creatures almost seemed as if they would force the fist open; but, finding it firmly shut, they flew up again in evident disappointment. After teasing them for a time, the man suddenly relaxed his grip. In a flash there was a whirr of white wings, and when I looked the bread was gone. Into my mind crept the lovely language of an old Hebrew poet: 'Thou openest Thine hand, and satisfiest the desire of every living thing,' (Psalm 145:16). Such is the general providence of God.

Side by side with this general providence, however, there is something more – a particular providence which extends exclusively to God's children. Surely it is only what might be expected that God should show a special concern for the members of His own spiritual family! Isaac Watts was certain that it is so. In a spacious hymn he makes the point splendidly:

'Thy providence is kind and large,
Both man and beast Thy bounty share;
The whole creation is Thy charge'

There you have the general providence of God asserted with sublime confidence. Yet Watts does not stop there. He goes on with a fourth line:
'But saints are Thy peculiar care.'

To put it otherwise, God accepts a special responsibility for the welfare of the members of His own family.

Once in a slummy district of London I happened to be in a small shop when two tiny girls – one aged about five, the other about three – came in together. 'Little Africans of our own breed,' their faces looked as if they hadn't had a wash for a month; their clothes were in tatters; their shoes were in shocking need of repair. Shuffling up to the counter, the older child placed a threepenny-piece on top of it and intimated that she wanted a lollipop. Now, it called for no arithmetical genius on my part to perceive that one lollipop was lamentably insufficient to meet the needs of TWO little girls; and instinctively I could not help feeling sorry for the younger child because it seemed her chances of a lick of the lollipop were extremely remote! Happily, behind the counter there was a kind heart. For the price of one, two lollipops were handed over; and I wish you could have seen the beatific beam on the grimy faces of those tiny tots as, each clutching a lollipop in a grubby fist, they made their way out of the shop. Watching them go, I felt a pang of sentimental pity for them. 'Somebody's unwanted children,' I mused, 'somebody's neglected family!' But suppose they had been MY children! Suppose they had borne my name and shared my life, what then? Why, then it would not just have been a pang of sentimental pity I should have felt for them. I should have considered myself personally responsible for their condition; I should have judged it my immediate duty to care and cater for them in a practical way; I should have seen to it that they were cleansed and clad and fed. In short, I should have accepted a special responsibility for them had they been my own.

Admittedly, the illustration is a poor one and must not be pressed too far. Nevertheless it does, I think, serve to bring out the truth I want here to make it plain – that God has a special and particular concern for His own children. 'Saints are His peculiar care.' Those who can truly say 'Our Father' are entitled, more than others, to go on to say, 'Give us this day our daily bread.' If, as Shakespeare maintains, there is a special providence in the fall of a sparrow, how much more special must be the providence sustaining those who are of more value than many sparrows?

There is the old Puritan's third point: SUPPORTED AND BROUGHT THROUGH.

TRANSPORTED AND BROUGHT HOME.

It seems to me that we modern preachers do not state nearly starkly enough the alternatives confronting men and women outside of Christ and insider of Christ. The alternatives are these: either a hole in the earth or a Home in heaven.

A hole in the earth! Apart from Jesus Christ – His teaching on the subject of immortality and His resurrection from the dead – what real certainty have we that anything awaits even the wisest and best of us but just that? As Thomas Gray's stately stanza expresses it:

'The boast of heraldry, the pomp of power,
And all that beauty, all that wealth e'er gave,
Awaits alike the inevitable hour-
The paths of glory lead but to the grave.'

Nor can the profoundest philosophy, the most penetrative science, produce compelling proof that a hole in the earth is not the final fate of man, and dust and ashes all that is. The tomb is a hungry mouth that swallows but does not speak, and that omnivorous and insatiable hole in the earth seems to threaten to devour us all.

On one occasion in Glasgow it was my unwelcome duty to officiate with a colleague at the funeral of a noted Communist leader. A flaming orator, he had spent his life going continuously from one part of the country to another, passionately propagating his political creed. In life he had been Karl Marx's man, every inch of him, and, in death, they had propped up the sagging jaw of his corpse with a huge copy of the Communist classic DAS KAPITAL. But as, on that bleak January day, I stood by his open grave on a snow-covered hillside, and saw the coffin being slowly lowered to its last resting-place, I was suddenly struck by the tragic irony of it all, and beneath my breath I muttered: 'Ah, poor fellow, of what use to you now are your Utopian dreams, your luring visions of an ideal social order, your conception of heaven as a Collectivist State in this world. Six feet of earth is all you'll have for ever!'

Do not misunderstand me. I am not denying the urgent need for schemes of social betterment. On the contrary, it seems to me that no man is awake to reality today who does not feel in his very bones that true Christianity is bound to present a tremendous challenge to the whole structure of society as now constituted, and that the bitterest irony of our time is that the loudest protest against the social and economic wrongs with which humanity is afflicted has come not from the GODLY but from the GODLESS! That is a terrible indictment of the Christian Church.

Nevertheless, the truth remains that no improvement in social conditions, the material setting of man's life, can ever permanently satisfy his immortal spirit, any more than a cheque for a million pounds could be of any personal consequence to a dying man.

Unless Christ was right about the future and unless He really rose from the dead, what are all our admirable plans for the amelioration of human conditions but so many designs for decorating a condemned cell? If there is nothing more than a hole in the earth ahead of us, what do such schemes ultimately matter after all?

'If!' But there is no 'if' about it! Christ is risen, and for those who love and trust Him He is preparing not a hole in the earth but a Home in heaven.

Years ago in Edinburgh an old saint lay dying. As the end drew near, his friends gathered round the bed and leaned over it to listen to the last utterance of his labouring breath, and this is what he said: 'I'm going Home as fast as I can, and I bless God I've a good Home to go to!' In the long run that is the only thing that really signifies.

Thus ends our brief survey of the four points of the old Puritan. 'He shall see His seed' – born and brought in, educated and brought up, supported and brought through, transported and brought Home.

God grant that we may all be gathered to that great Home at last; that, if I may slightly alter and adapt some lovely lines, as

'All things rest at eventide,
Like birds that weary of their roaming,
So we shall hasten to His side,
Homing.'

🌿 Donald MacFarlane

Donald MacFarlane was born in 1834 in the island of North Uist, Scotland. It was while listening to a sermon preached by the Rev. Alexander MacColl that the Holy Spirit convicted him of his need of Christ and he accepted Him at the age of twenty-two. After studying at Glasgow University and the Free Church College, he was then licensed to preach and in 1876 he was inducted as the minister of Strathconan Free Church. This was followed by successful ministries in the Moy and Raasay congregations and in 1903 he accepted a call from the Dingwall congregation, where he continued to preach until his death in 1926.

Donald Beaton, his biographer, wrote the following:- 'He shunned not to declare the whole counsel of God. He believed the Bible to be the Word of God with all his heart; he received its truths unhesitatingly, and whether these were popular or unpopular with men never weighed with him as a servant of Christ. He never forgot in his preaching that he was only a servant in the Master's house, that the message was not his, but that of Him whom he served.'

This message is from the book SERMONS BY REV. DONALD MACFARLAND first published in 1918.

Chapter ten

CHRIST SEEING OF HIS TRAVAIL

'HE SHALL SEE OF THE TRAVAIL OF HIS SOUL, AND SHALL BE SATISFIED: BY HIS
KNOWLEDGE SHALL MY RIGHTEOUS SERVANT JUSTIFY MANY; FOR HE SHALL BEAR
THEIR INIQUITIES.' – ISAIAH 53:11

THERE IS AN INTIMATE CONNECTION BETWEEN THE 53ᴿᴰ, 54ᵀᴴ,
AND 55ᵀᴴ CHAPTERS OF THIS PROPHECY. THE 53ᴿᴰ SPEAKS OF
the sufferings of Christ; the 54ᵗʰ, of the fruit of His sufferings; and the
55ᵗʰ, of the call of the Gospel to gather sinners to Him. Our text speaks of
His sufferings, and also of the fruit of His suffering.

In speaking on this subject, we shall notice-

i)   THE SOUL TRAVAIL OF CHRIST

ii) THE FRUIT OF IT

iii) THAT HE SHALL BE SATISFIED WITH THE FRUIT OF HIS SOUL
     TRAVAIL

i) THE SOUL TRAVAIL OF CHRIST

Christ assumed the whole of man's nature – soul and body, and suffered in both, though here it is only His soul that is mentioned. Though the sufferings of His body were great, His sufferings were much greater and most severe to endure. It is well known by experience among men in all generations that mental or soul trouble is more difficult to endure than bodily trouble. The soul of Christ is mentioned in the text to indicate the magnitude of His sufferings. He lays emphasis on this Himself when He says, 'My soul is exceeding sorrowful unto death.' By His sufferings in soul and body, which He finished by His death on the cross, He obtained everlasting redemption for His people.

ii) THE FRUIT OF HIS SUFFERINGS: 'HE SHALL SEE OF THE TRAVAIL OF HIS SOUL.'

Christ's soul travail shall not be in vain; it shall yield abundant fruit, which shall be to the glory of God, and the good of men. This is made certain in scripture. 'Verily, verily, I say unto you, except a corn of wheat fall into the ground and die, it abideth alone: but if it die, it bringeth forth much fruit' John 12:24). Many other passages of Scripture speak to the same effect. The time of Christ's sufferings was the time in which He sowed, and afterwards came the time of His reaping. He sowed in tears, He reaps with joy. Let us notice some of the most important fruits that spring from His sufferings:

1   The satisfying of God's law, which was violated by man. Christ rendered full satisfaction to the law in its precept and penalty by His obedience unto death. The typical sacrifices could never do this, hence they had to be offered up from year to year for the space of 4000 years, till Christ came. But He, by the one offering of Himself satisfied all the requirements of the law. It does not need more; yea, it does not accept more. The typical sacrifices were repeated because of their imperfection and their inability to take away sin: the sacrifice of Christ is not to be repeated because of its perfection. 'He offered

Himself once' – once for all. To offer up Christ again, as some pretend to do,, would be an insult to heaven, an insult to the justice of God, and an insult to Christ, who cried, triumphantly, 'It is finished.'

2   The glory of God is another great fruit. 'I have glorified Thee on the earth.' He did so by His finished work. 'I have finished the work which Thou gavest Me to do.' Man by sin dishonoured God. How can he make amends for this? He can never do it in his own person. But here is his remedy – Christ, as the glorious Substitute of the sinner, glorified the Father by His sufferings. He rendered glory to God with large interest, so that God has now more glory in the salvation of the sinner – the chief of sinners – than He could ever have if man had never sinned or fallen. What an encouragement this is to poor sinners who are afraid that God will not save them because of the dishonour they have cast upon Him. Poor soul, God shall have no loss of glory in your salvation if you come to Him by Christ who glorified Him; yea, He will have more glory, as we have said, than if you had never offended Him by your sins!

4   Another fruit is eternal life. Christ did two things by His sufferings:–
l)   He satisfied the law, for the breach of it by sin.
2)   He merited eternal life.

He paid the debt, and at the same time purchased the blessings of salvation. The value of His work arises from the dignity of His Person as the God-man. God is surely more satisfied with Christ's atonement than He could be with the sinner though he were able to make atonement in his own person. This is the greatest encouragement to convinced sinners to come as they are to God by Christ, pleading His merits. Let not, then, your sins, however great, keep you back from coming. The devil would drive you to despair, for he has no gospel, but God bids you come to Him, and assures you that though your sins are as scarlet, and red like crimson, they shall be white as wool, 'For the blood of Jesus Christ, His Son, cleanseth from all sin' I John I:7.

5   Another fruit is the ingathering of sinners to Christ, and their conversion to God. 'He shall see His seed.' 'And I, if I be lifted up from the earth, will draw all men unto Me.' This is to be accomplished by the preaching of the Gospel, and the outpouring of the Holy Spirit, and His saving work in the souls of sinners. For this end God set up the Gospel ministry in His Church on earth. It shall answer, without fail, God's purpose as a means of grace and salvation. Let us notice this fruit and effect on the travail of Christ's soul:

1)   Christ saw the fruit of His redemption before He suffered. For the space of 4000 years He was gathering in from generation to generation this kind of fruit. God gave a long credit to His Son on the ground of His promise before He actually paid the price of the redemption of His people. Christ's promise of working out redemption was accepted of the Father, knowing that He who promised was faithful to fulfil it. All the Old Testament believers received salvation on the ground of that promise. They received grace and glory.

     The first of this kind of fruit was Abel, and probably his parents – Adam and Eve. Abel was the first of the human race that entered heaven. For his entering that glorious place he must have been a sight to the holy angels, who desire with delight to look into this redemption, and who rejoice at the repentance of even one sinner. And his own wonder and joy could be no less than that of the happy company he joined. Though the only solitary creature of a different race there, he felt himself at home in his Father's house. He could sing a song which the angels that never sinned could not sing. He was the first martyr, and the first to receive the crown. He received the crown, not on the ground of his own blood, which was shed for his faith in Christ, but on the ground of the blood of Christ, that was shadowed forth in the bloody sacrifice he offered up to God. This was the first ripe fruit Christ gathered in as the fruit of His soul travail. More fruit shall follow. It is only the beginning of the great harvest. 'Ye shall see greater things than these.'

From Abel to the time of the Flood the true religion ran in the line of the posterity of Seth, while the posterity of Cain, the persecutor and murderer, were left without the fear of God, and were practical atheists, if not professedly so. At the time when Enos was born, and for a considerable time thereafter, it appears that there was a large outpouring of the Spirit of grace and supplication, and a great revival of religion took place, for it is said, 'Then began men to call on the name of the Lord' Genesis 4:26. There were praying people before then, but it would appear that now the number was largely increased. The true worship of God, of which prayer is an important part, was general, and it is supposed that at this time many families assembled together to worship publicly as a congregation. This is highly probable, as there is such notice taken of this time in Scripture. 'Then men began to call upon the name of the Lord.' Though it is only the principal men of that age whose names are given as possessed of true piety, yet we may well believe that Christ gathered in a large harvest in that generation as the fruit of the travail of His soul. Many shall be seen in heaven whose names are not mentioned either in the Bible or in Church History.

At the time of the Flood, Christ's flock was very small, but there was a remnant. Noah alone is mentioned as having found favour or grace in the sight of the Lord. As the effect of that favour he was righteous, and as the effect of his being righteous 'he walked with God.' While God was provoked to sweep away from the face of the earth that wicked generation of men, He took good care to preserve a seed from which Christ should see in after ages to the end of the world more abundantly of the travail of His soul than He had hitherto seen. There were in the ark representatives of all future nations. Shem, Ham, and Japeth were the seed that was to take root, spring up, and fill the world with human beings. Christ shall see of the travail of His soul among the peoples and nations of the earth. Though Ham was wicked, yet the command was, 'Destroy him not,' for some, yea, many of his posterity were to be saved. He was spared because Christ would see the travail of His soul in his posterity, however remote. Wicked people are spared for the same reason. From the Flood, to the time of the giving of the law through Moses, the true religion still ran in the line of Shem, one of Noah's sons, and a direct descendant of Seth.

During that period Christ saw much of the travail of His soul. Among the rich harvest He reaped saved persons, we find some who were head and shoulders above others in eminent piety and usefulness, such as Abraham, Isaac, and Jacob, and from Jacob sprang the twelve tribes of Israel. The promise of the coming Messiah was renewed to these patriarchs successively in their respective generations; and as the Gospel was thus preached to them, it may on good grounds be believed that many were gathered into the fold of Christ as the fruit of travail of His soul.

During the sojourn of Israel in Egypt they had many tokens of the Lord's lovingkindness, and the true religion was kept alive and shone in the midst of the darkness by which it was surrounded. They were brought into that heathen country in a very mysterious manner, and their deliverance out of it was marvellous.

'It was the doing of the Lord, and wondrous in our eyes,' and so it is in ours. Notwithstanding the decay that true piety had undergone in this idolatrous kingdom, Christ saw of the travail of His soul to some extent among them. When the Lord delivered the people out of their bondage in Egypt, the true religion was revived and firmly established in a manner which it had not hitherto attained. The people were formed into a nation, and organised into one congregation to worship the Lord at one place of worship – the Tabernacle. A written law was given them to guide and regulate them in their duties to God and man. The moral law, which was of binding obligation, was designed to remind them of their sinfulness, to deter them from sin, and to show that by the deeds of the law no flesh could be justified in the sight of God. The ceremonial law, which was only temporary, showed them the way of salvation by the blood of Christ, of which the bloody sacrifices were a type, and the civil law was meant to guide them in their civil transactions with one another and with their heathen neighbours. So far as these laws were concerned, everything was now complete. At this time God entered into a covenant with them, and they by profession complied with the covenant. Though many of them broke the covenant, yet Christ saw of the travail of His soul in a considerable number of them, especially among the young that came out of Egypt, and others that were born in the wilderness. All that came out of Egypt, except two – Caleb and Joshua – died in the wilderness. Their children entered the promised land. The exclusion of the great bulk of the rest was because of their unbelief (Hebrews 3:9). Some, however, who died there, died in the faith and entered heaven. Among these were Aaron and Moses and others. Christ had seen a gleaning among them.

When the Lord brought the people of Israel into the land of Canaan according to His promise, with Caleb and Joshua of the old generation at their head, and settled them in their inheritances, the true religion advanced and made more progress than it had hitherto done. It is probable that Christ had reaped a large harvest from among the young generation that were brought across the Jordan in such a miraculous manner. In the time of the Judges, religion had its ups and downs; but even then we find among the people some who were stars of the first magnitude. The tribe of Judah appears to be prominent in this respect. And in the time of the Kings, up to the revolt of the ten tribes under 'Jeroboam, who made Israel to sin,' the true religion prospered considerably, and Christ saw of the travail of His soul very largely. It got an impetus when David began to reign, and went on prospering during his lifetime, and afterwards it was he that brought the ark that wandered, for a short time in the land of the Philistines, and for a much longer time in the land of Israel, to its resting place in Jerusalem.

During the greater part of Solomon's reign the Lord's cause was advancing more and more, but towards the end of his reign it was marred by the countenance he gave to idolatry. Though he was brought to repentance, the evil he did in this respect was visited with the Lord's displeasure and judgment, by rending the kingdom in the beginning of the reign of his son, Rehoboam, which resulted in the revolt of the ten tribes. This division continued till the captivity. Sin is the cause of division in the visible church. If all adhered to God and the rule of His word there would be no division. Jeroboam was given as king, like Saul, in God's anger, and the kings of Israel that succeeded him bore the same stigma. The kings of Judah, though not perfect, were, as a rule, godly and good kings. It was in their line that true religion was kept pure, till toward the end they fell into the mire of idolatry as deep as Israel, or deeper, and they followed Israel into captivity in Babylon, where for seventy long years they saw and bitterly felt the error of their ways, and learnt to say, 'What have I to do any more with idols?' They were sent into captivity that they might see that it was an evil and bitter thing to have forsaken the Lord. The Lord did not utterly forsake them there, though they forsook Him. It was a token for good that He had some of His prophets with them in their banishment.

When they were, in God's good providence, brought back from captivity, the Lord's CAUSE was revived. The division between Judah and Israel came to an end. All that came back went by the name of JEWS. The two parties – Israel and Judah – were melted in the furnace, and they were now blended into one party. Some will be for contriving methods for healing the divisions that are in the visible church. Many methods are proposed, but TRUE REPENTANCE is that which succeeds in bringing the different sections of the Church together. There must be first a return to God and His word, and then a union between themselves will easily follow as the result.

A great revival of religion followed the deliverance from the captivity. The temple, which was so long in ashes, was rebuilt, the walls of Jerusalem were repaired, the worship of God was set up, and many sinners were converted and built up in the faith, and thus Christ saw much of His soul travail. It was the glory of the second temple that the Messiah Himself came to it, not in type as in the first temple, but personally in human nature. 'God was manifested in the flesh.' The Church, which shone with such glorious lustre at and for some time after the rebuilding of the temple, was so benighted with unbelief and error that the Jews did not know their long looked for Messiah when He came. But there was a remnant among them that knew Him, and hailed His coming with delight. These were a seed from which Christ was in due time to reap a rich harvest. 'He shall see of the travail of His soul.'

This is a faithful promise, and is sure to be fulfilled. This fact is a strong evidence of the truth of Scripture. The promise of Christ's first coming took 4000 years in its accomplishment, but it was fulfilled, and so will all the other promises in the Bible be fulfilled.

Christ was seeing of the travail of His soul during His state of humiliation. He was sowing and reaping at the same time. It was then He called and gathered around Him those whom He afterwards, after His resurrection, sent forth as His apostles to preach the Gospel to all nations and to add to the canon of Scripture. It is a good sign in any age when Christ raises up Gospel ministers in His Church, though the number of other converts be small. It is a sign that He has a work for them to do, and that He will bless their labours.

Christ saw of the travail of His soul after He finished the work of redemption. He got the salvation of the Old Testament believers on the credit of His promise to finish the work. He gets the salvation of the New Testament believers, not on credit, but on the actual payment of the debt and the meriting of their salvation. The day of Pentecost was the beginning of the great harvest in this respect. Three thousand were gathered into His fold by means of one sermon preached by Peter. The Apostles went forth and preached everywhere, and there were numbers converted and added to the Church, even as many as should be saved. It would appear that every sermon was blessed to some. The word of the Lord was used in the conversion of each and all. We have no record of any being converted without God's word, which is a strong argument against those who maintain that the heathen may be converted to God without the Gospel. 'How shall they believe in Him of whom they have not heard?' The Apostle's question implies an impossibility, and he spoke by the inspiration of the Holy Spirit. 'To the law and to the testimony, if they speak not according to it, it is because there is no light in them.' 'The Gospel is the power of God unto salvation to every one that believeth, to the Jew first, and to the Gentile also.' During the Apostles' lifetime Christ reaped an abundant harvest of souls by the means of their preaching. They preached the Gospel throughout the most at least of the Roman dominions, which then included the known world, and gathered as instruments many sinners – Jews and Gentiles – to the fold of Christ.

In the first century after the death of the Apostle John – the last of the Apostles – errors began to creep into the Church. The first of the apostolic fathers, who saw and heard the Apostles, kept in the main sound in the faith, but the fathers that succeeded these brought errors into the Church, which were added to from time to time thereafter, till the predicted great apostasy came to a height in the 7th century. The light of the Gospel was then put under a bushel, and darkness covered the earth, and gross darkness the people. The light of the Gospel was not, however, extinguished in the world. It shone brightly in some corners of the earth. It shone in some parts of France, Switzerland, and even in some parts of the Highlands of Scotland. When thick darkness covered the Egyptians in Egypt, the people of Israel had light in Goshen where they dwelt. So it was during the 'Dark Ages.' The Gospel is like the sun that always shines somewhere in the world, and like the fire that came down from heaven to burn the sacrifice: it never went out till Christ came. The Gospel shall continue to shine in the world till Christ comes again. It shall answer the end for which it was sent to us. By means of it Christ shall see of the travail of His soul. 'It shall not return unto Me void, but it shall accomplish that which I please, and it shall prosper in the thing whereto I sent it' (Isaiah 55:11).

At the time of the Reformation in the 16th century the Gospel began to shine more brightly, and to diffuse its light more widely throughout the kingdoms of Europe, dispelling the darkness that so long covered these countries. 'He shall see of the travail of His soul.'

iii)   THAT HE SHALL BE SATISFIED WITH THE FRUIT OF HIS SOUL TRAVAIL.

He shall be so satisfied that He shall not receive any addition to the number of the saved. The door of mercy shall be shut forever, and although some would knock at that door, it shall never be opened. All the members of the mystical body of Christ are gathered in and united to Him. The Church which is His body is said to be the fullness of Christ (Ephesians 4:13).

It will take to the end of the world till all shall be taken in. Then the world itself, which some compare to a scaffolding set up to a house when building, and taken down when the house is finished – the world itself shall be reduced to nothing when the spiritual building is completed. This is the day of our opportunity, and the Gospel calls upon sinners to come to Christ to be saved; but the call stops at death, it will not follow sinners into eternity. As it was in this world that Christ finished the work of redemption , it is in this world that the redemption is applied to those that believe in Christ. Seek, then, the Holy Spirit to apply the redemption to you, and seek the Lord while He is to be found, and call upon Him while He is near. AMEN.

🌿 T. T. Shields

T. T. Shields was born in Bristol, England in 1873, the son of a Baptist minister. He was converted to Christ as a young man and upon completion of his studies he was ordained to the Baptist ministry in 1897. Following this he pastored four churches in Ontario and in 1910 he was called to the famous Jarvis Street Baptist Church in Toronto. He founded THE GOSPEL WITNESS magazine in 1922 and was named by Sir W. R. Nicol who was the editor of THE BRITISH WEEKLY as 'The Canadian Spurgeon.' In 1927 he established the Toronto Baptist Seminary, and for many years he was president of the Union of Regular Baptist Churches of Ontario and Quebec.

It was said of him that he was a master interpreter of the Bible, and each time he expounded the Scriptures there was something fresh and original.

He was the author of several books and booklets and this sermon is taken from the book CHRIST IN THE OLD TESTAMENT.

Chapter eleven

HE HATH POURED OUT HIS SOUL UNTO DEATH

'THEREFORE WILL I DIVIDE HIM A PORTION WITH THE GREAT, AND HE SHALL
DIVIDE THE SPOIL WITH THE STRONG; BECAUSE HE HATH POURED OUT HIS SOUL
UNTO DEATH: AND HE WAS NUMBERED WITH THE TRANSGRESSORS; AND HE
BARE THE SIN OF MANY, AND MADE INTERCESSION FOR THE TRANSGRESSORS.'
— ISAIAH 53:12

THERE IS NO PASSAGE IN THE WORD OF GOD WHICH DOES NOT
BEAR A DEFINITE RELATION TO THE DEATH OF CHRIST, AND TO
all that is involved in that tremendous, historic event. Therefore, all
sermons, all preaching, ought to be directly related to the Cross. It is a
subject which no one can possibly exhaust. No one has ever scaled the
heights, nor fathomed the depths, nor explored the infinite fullness, of
that great mystery of the manifestation of God in the flesh.

Such a text as this would require ages to expound — indeed, the
experience of millennia would be necessary properly to understand it. Yet
though we may not understand it all, nor have the ability to expound the
little we understand, it may be profitable for us to walk about this vast
storehouse of truth, and at least gaze upon it in the hope that some day,

by God's good pleasure, in the ages to come wherein He will show us 'the exceeding riches of his grace in his kindness towards us through Christ Jesus,' we may better understand the significance of the death of Christ.

ONE

To come to the text at once, it suggests that THE PHYSICAL DEATH OF OUR LORD JESUS WAS REALLY THE CULMINATION OF HIS SOUL-AGONY: 'He poured out His soul unto death.' What contracted views men entertain of the cross of Christ! How superficial is our understanding of its significance! We speak of its physical elements, the cross of wood, the wounds in His body, the physical suffering occasioned by them. I have heard a hymn about 'the old rugged cross.' As a symbol, it has its value. But there is more than an instrument of torture and of death in the cross.

The physical sufferings of our Lord Jesus, the piercing of His hands and feet with the nails, the pressing upon His brow of the crown of thorns, and the driving to His heart of the soldier's spear, were a spectacle dreadful to contemplate. Assuredly the physical sufferings of our Lord were very great; but our text relates to His physical suffering only in a subordinate sense: it refers to the agony of His infinite soul, and tells us that His death, that physical fact when the heart ceased to beat, the blood to course through the veins, and the pulse to throb, as He bowed His head and gave up the ghost – that that physical fact was but the climax of a long-drawn-out agony of a soul that was infinite in its capacity: 'He poured out his soul unto death.'

I think we may remind ourselves THAT PHYSICAL DEATH IS NOT ALWAYS ASSOCIATED WITH ANGUISH OF SOUL. There may be physical death, indeed, without the slightest mental torture. When life is suddenly terminated, when in a moment, in the twinkling of an eye, the heart is stilled, there is no anguish of soul. But death is still real in such a case. Sometimes we have seen an aged man, or woman, patiently waiting for the call; and when at length death came there was no anguish. It was like Tennyson's beautiful description of the close of life's day:

'Sunset and evening star,
And one clear call for me!
And may there be no moaning of the bar,
When I put out to sea,
'But such a tide as moving seems asleep,
Too full for sound and foam,
When that which drew from out the boundless deep
Turns again home.'

The soul departs without any turbulency of mind, only a quiet falling upon sleep. Yet the fact of physical death is not less real.

Sometimes we have observed such a departure in the case of one whose life had not been fully lived, but whose energies had been sapped by some fell disease, but who was prepared for passage to another life. Such a one was willing to depart, and to be with Christ 'which is far better;' and when at last the silver cord was loosed, and the golden bowl broken, when the pitcher was broken at the fountain, and the wheel broken at the cistern, when the spirit returned unto God who gave it, and man departed for his long home, there was an element of gladness about it. The advent of the grim messenger was rather welcome as heralding deliverance from pain, as a realisation of the believer's desire.

'Twilight and evening bell,
And after that the dark!
And may there be no sadness of farewell,
When I embark;
'For tho' from out our bourne of Time and Place
The flood may bear me far,
I hope to see my Pilot face to face
When I have crost the bar.'

No; physical death does not always involve agony of soul.

NOR CAN WE SAY THAT THE DEATH OF THE LORD JESUS, PHYSICALLY, WAS OF ALL DEATHS THE MOST PAINFUL. It was painful, but there were others who died

with Him; one on either side, crucified as was He. And when death came
to them, it came to bodies that were not sinless; and therefore one might
suppose had less power of resistance than the sinless body of the Lord
Jesus. Doubtless He suffered – of course He did. Crucifixion was
designed to be a slow and painful death. But many have died amid
circumstances more trying than did Jesus on the cross. Read the eleventh
chapter of Hebrews, where the roll of the heroes of faith is called, of
those who were stoned, sawn asunder, tortured of beasts, consumed in
the flames. Many of the martyrs suffered more physically than did the
Lord Jesus.

I think I may state more positively, that by virtue of the fact that His
body was without taint of sin, His body must have been the more
invulnerable, and less susceptible to the attacks of disease, better
fortified against the approach of death, than either of the thieves who
died with Him. And yet He died first. When the soldiers came to those
who were crucified, and found the thieves still living, that their bodies
might not remain on the cross over the Sabbath, they brake their legs to
hasten their death. But when they came to Jesus they found that He was
dead already. That splendid frame, the most perfect human physique the
world had ever seen, judged by all true standards, succumbed before the
enfeebled bodies of the malefactors who were crucified with Him.

What killed Him? 'He poured out His soul unto death.' Is it not clear
that the death of the Lord Jesus was THE CULMINATION OF AN AGE-LONG
ANTICIPATION OF THE AGONY OF THAT HOUR? It was not until He was
comparatively near the cross that Jesus began to say to His disciples that
the Son of man would be betrayed into the hands of sinners, and that He
would die at Jerusalem. He withheld the revelation of that Divine purpose
from those who were His companions, not for His own sake, but for
theirs; in agreement with the principle expressed on another occasion, 'I
have yet many things to say unto you, but ye cannot bear them now.' Had
He told them at the beginning of the three years of their discipleship,
they could not have borne it. But HE bore it! HE knew the particulars of
that anguished hour from all eternity.

Here it is in Isaiah's prophecy, long, long years before 'Jesus was born
in Bethlehem of Judaea in the days of Herod the king.' If you go back still

farther into history, to the days of David, you will find Him, through the lips of David, prophetically crying, 'My God, my God, why hast thou forsaken me?' They very words that He uttered while hanging on the cross found prophetic statement through one to whom the vision was given centuries before. And long before that – before He gave to the sea His decree that the waters should not pass His commandment, before He laid the foundations of the earth, before He stretched out the firmament as a tent to dwell in, before He placed therein the myriad stars, or kindled the two great lamps to light this earthly house by night and day, even long before He said, 'Let us make man in our image, after our likeness' – from before the foundation of the world the Lamb was slain. And through all succeeding ages He lived in anticipation of the agony of that dark hour when He should make His soul an offering for sin. When the fullness of time was come He took on Him our flesh, was manifest among men, He went to the cross, He bowed His head and gave up the ghost – He died there physically. But I say, it was the culmination of millennia of anticipation. You must not confine the sufferings of Christ to a few hours of time. The sins of this world were not atoned for by a few hours of superlative grief. Reconciliation was not effected by the sorrows of those hours of darkness, even though the capacity of the soul of Him Who there suffered was infinite. No! No! Jesus Christ always suffered! He suffered from eternity! He was the suffering God! He took upon Himself the sorrows of the world.

I suppose, too, that that PHYSICAL DEATH WAS THE CLIMAX OF THE SOUL-TORTURE WHICH WAS THE INEVITABLE CONCOMITANT OF HIS CONTACT WITH SIN. How His holy soul must have shrunk from contact with that sin that is so vile that it is described as the 'abominable thing which God hates.' I have been in places where I have suffered greater mental discomfort than any physical discomfort to which I have been exposed. It was my fate on one occasion to eat dinner in a certain place – or to try to do so. I have never forgotten it. It was an uncomfortable hour.

I was in a certain Western city some years ago, when every day a new restaurant was being opened. I was there for a holiday, and about lunch time I walked about to try to find a good restaurant. I entered one of the new restaurants. It was a hot day in summer; they had no screens; and I concluded that all the flies of Egypt had emigrated! They were all there. I entered, looked around, and a very polite man said, 'What can we do for you, sir?' 'Nothing thank you,' I said, and I left more quickly that I entered.

Sometimes we are very particular. WE are very particular! WE, vile sinners that we are! We set up our standards, and look down as though from an immeasurable height upon somebody we esteem to be our inferior. It is not always comfortable to be forced to occupy certain positions, to find oneself in certain situations. I have been in company that I did not like. Please do not say that I was unspiritual because I did not like the company. There are a few people I do not find it easy to like. By the grace of God, I hope I can love them; but there are people for whom I have no natural affinity. I should not like to live with them. We have nothing in common on any plane. There may be some superior gentleman back there who says, 'That is mutual, sir.' Very well. I shall not complain. We are entitled to our likes and dislikes, I suppose. But howsoever refined a man may be in the habits of his physical life, the food he eats, the raiment he wears, the house he lives in, and his attention to the niceties of a comfortable existence – however refined he may be, what does he know about true refinement?

Mentally refined? What are you, a Master of Arts? A Doctor of Philosophy? What science do you know? What languages? What literature? What acquaintance have you with the great earth? The inhabitants of the earth are reckoned as grasshoppers to Him Who sitteth upon the circle of the earth: 'For thus saith the high and lofty One that inhabiteth eternity, whose name is Holy; I dwell in the high and holy place, with him also that is of a contrite and humble spirit, to revive the spirit of the humble, and to revive the heart of the contrite ones.' It is He of Whom I speak. He stooped and came into contact with sin. How it must have afflicted His exquisitely sensitive soul! How it must have tortured Him to be in its presence! Of purer eyes than to behold evil, He could not look upon iniquity.

'He poured out His soul unto death.' He 'was made sin for us.' I am only trying to show you how impossible it is for any finite mind to fathom its depths: 'He poured out HIS soul unto death.' 'HIS soul'! What was 'HIS soul'? The soul of the Infinite, every quality of which was in the infinite and absolute degree, was 'poured out unto death'! The cross was the climax the end of the out-pouring of His infinite soul. It was poured out not BY death, but UNTO death. That was the acme, the ultimate, of Divine anguish.

I suppose, too, that ALIENATION FROM GOD, THE SENSE OF SEPARATION FROM THE FATHER, MUST HAVE BEEN AN ELEMENT IN THE EXQUISITE AGONY THAT FOUND ITS EXPRESSION IN THE TWENTY-SECOND PSALM I QUOTED A FEW MOMENTS AGO, 'My God, my God, why hast thou forsaken me?' God was His very life. He was one with the Father and the Holy Ghost. He spoke of the glory which He had with the Father 'before the worlds were.' But even then, in that immeasurably remote and dateless past His perceptive and responsive soul shuddered in anticipation of the horror of thick darkness incident to His separation from God.

When someone suddenly faints in a building, how people rush to his aid! They open windows and doors, to give the sufferer contact with fresh air, that nothing may obstruct his breathing, that he may have full, free, and unfettered correspondence with that vital environment which is necessary to life. But the Lord Jesus was separated from God. I do not understand it. Nobody knows what it meant to this infinitely holy Soul to be separated from God, to be separated by the world's sin; to be 'made sin,' to have sin in the mass, sin in all its heinousness, in all its ugliness, in all its vastness, its immensity, between Him and God. How great must the torture of the Soul that suffered thus have been, when His was the soul of the Infinite!

But OUR LORD'S SEPARATION FROM THE FATHER INVOLVED MORE THAN FORSAKENESS. It must have involved a sense of Divine displeasure. No sinful, mortal man could even imagine the exquisite torture, His divinely sensitive soul must have suffered as the Lord 'laid upon him the iniquity of us all,' and He was therefore bruised of the Lord, and put to grief. Himself the Holy One, it must have been the equivalent of a thousand hells to feel Himself abhorred by Divine Holiness. His incomparably sensitive, because absolutely holy, soul must have writhed in anguished horror in the consciousness of it.

There is something in the figure employed: 'He poured out his soul unto death.' As though the elements of His soul – shall I seem to be crude, too realistic, if I say that the figure suggests that the elements of His soul had somehow been molten, as though the vital energies had been melted in the fires of Divine wrath. I have seen life ebbing away from a physical frame, and have heard the doctor to the anxious enquiry of a relative, 'What is the prospect, doctor?' answer, 'I cannot say. He may not last the night, and he may last several days. Physically, I should have expected the patient to slip out before this; but he has a strong will, and is making a valiant fight.' How often you have read that of certain people! They fought the last great enemy. They were determined to live, and they co-operated with all healing processes that were set in operation, with all healing ministries that were exercised in their behalf. By that thing that is not physical, the will, the heart was stimulated, and it beat on. The body was bouyed up. But at last the toxins reached the brain, the mind ceased to function, the will surrendered, became quiescent, and soon all resistance subsided, death ensued.

'He poured out his soul unto death.' Who knoweth the mind of the Lord? Who would dare, without irreverence, to attempt an analysis of the mind of God? Think of all the qualities of that Soul, the vital energies resident in the unique personality of the Lord Jesus! But at last – at last – drop by drop, He pours it out until the last drop of vital energy is poured out, spent, and death ensues: 'Unto death!' Even the God-man, under that exquisite, indescribable, inexpressible, agony that grew out of His relation to the world's sin, and His separation from God - at last that incalculable weight crushed His spirit, and the last drop of His energy was pressed out, like wine in the wine vat. The breast ceased to heave, and He yielded up His spirit. He died because His soul had exhausted itself with the sorrows of a world.

TWO

Let us now take a step father and observe that THE PHYSICAL DEATH OF JESUS WAS A REVELATION OF ITS MORAL PURPOSE.

Why did He die? 'He was numbered with the transgressors.' That was LITERALLY AND HISTORICALLY A FACT. Two malefactors were crucified with Him that it might be fulfilled which was spoken by the Scripture, 'He was numbered with the transgressors.' But what was implied in that? He put on Him a convict's garb. He was made in the likeness of sinful flesh. He came i nto the prison-house, just as Joseph was cast into Potiphar's prison. He stood before the bar of human judgment, and was declared to be worthy of death. They took Him at last to the cross, as though He were a common malefactor. So fully did He identify Himself with humankind, that He even died as a transgressor. It was but a physical manifestation of the great spiritual fact that Jesus Christ took upon Himself our nature, in order that He might identify Himself with us, and be 'numbered with the transgressors.' He trod the common earth with us, He was born as we are born; He laboured as we must labour; He died at last as we must die. But behind it all is the fact that He came to be our Substitute, to take His place with us: 'When the fullness of the time was come, God sent forth His Son, made of a woman, made under the law, to redeem them that were under the law, that we might receive the adoption of sons.' 'He was numbered with the transgressors.'

'AND HE BARE THE SIN OF MANY.' I try to tell you that in some form every time I preach, but I must tell you again. I do not know what it means. I know its results. But what do you know about it. though you have heard it ten thousand times? 'He bare the sin of many.' Yet He was sinless, holy as God is holy; but "he bare the sin of many." That great truth, dear friends, is generally denied in our day. How seldom is that central fact proclaimed – or even believed – by professing Christians, that Jesus was in some mysterious way our Representative, that He did actually take upon Himself our sins, that He bare our sins in His own body on the tree, and that when He died, He did render to the holy law of God a just equivalent for our sin, that He paid the utmost farthing of the penalty our sin had incurred! Say it over a million times, 'He bare the sin of many.' There could be no salvation for any one of us but for that fact: He bare our sin, your sin and mine. I cannot tell you the weight of it. I cannot tell you what was involved, but He bore stripe for stripe, stroke for stroke, wound for wound, eye for eye, tooth for tooth, life for life. He gave His life instead of yours; instead of mine: 'He poured out his soul unto death;' and in the doing of it, He 'bare the sin of many.'

Are you not glad your debt is paid? There is no other chance of deliverance that that, nor is there any possibility of loss to the soul whose sin He bore.

'AND MADE INTERCESSION FOR THE TRANSGRESSORS.' We might not have understood what that meant if He had not made perfect intercession actually on the cross. Even as He was pouring out His soul unto death. He cried, 'Father forgive them; for they know not what they do.' For whom did He pray? 'For the chief priests and the scribes – for all that rabble crew who said, 'Away with Him! Crucify Him? He is not fit to live.' For those who know Him not, 'for had they known it they would not have crucified the Lord of glory.' But they did crucify Him. And for the soldiers, too, the very men who drove the nails, for all who participated in that crucifixion – for every one of them Jesus Christ prayed, 'father, forgive them; for they know not what they do.'

Let me for once give my testimony. I know I am a great sinner. But I cannot conceive of any way by which I could commit a greater sin than by swearing away the life of the Man of Galilee, by denying His Deity, by demanding His blood, by putting a crown of thorns about His brow, driving nails through His hands and feet, spitting in His face, mocking Him, and exposing Him to the contempt of a world. I could not commit any greater sin than that. Who could sin more heinously? But alas! I did that! My sin did that! And even as I did it, He said, 'Father, forgive him; for he knows not what he does.' He has been praying for me ever since, and He is praying for me now. I do not understand why He should do so, but He does. And He is praying for you: 'He made intercession for the transgressors.'

> 'I have a Saviour, He's pleading in glory,
> A dear loving saviour, though earth-friends be few;
> And now He is watching in tenderness o'er me,
> And, oh, that my Saviour were your Saviour too!'

THREE

Suffer this word, but how shall I speak it? It transcends our utmost thought when we attempt an exposition of it. On the basis of His pouring out His soul unto death, His being numbered with the transgressors, His bearing the sin of many, His making intercession for the transgressors, the Holy One speaks, 'Therefore I will divide him a portion with the great, and he shall divide the spoil with the strong.' THE DEATH OF THE LORD JESUS IS THE GROUND OF HIS SUPREMEST GLORY. He is to have 'a portion with the great.' And who are the 'great'? Where are they? Does it mean with the mighty of the earth? There is probably here an accommodation to human standards, as when Divine qualities are compared with such qualities in lesser degree in men. He was 'the firstborn from the dead, that in all things he might have the pre-eminence.' Thus above all the great of the earth, He has also a portion with Him Who is the Almighty, one with God forevermore. He hath put all things under His feet. By reason of the victory of the cross He will divide Him a portion with the great: 'Wherefore God also hath highly exalted him, and given him a name that is above every name: that at the name of Jesus every knee should bow, of things in heaven, and things in earth and things under the earth; and that every tongue should confess that Jesus Christ is Lord, to the glory of God the Father.' I quote that text to myself very often when I read books by little men who think they can measure the Lord Jesus Christ, who rob Him of His Deity, and circumscribe His person, reducing Him to the level of a man by comparing Him with men. Blessed be God, He has given Him a name that is above every name; and sooner or later at the name of Jesus every knee shall bow, and 'every tongue confess that Jesus Christ is Lord, to the glory of God the Father.'

How I wish I had skill, and time to exercise the skill, to tell you something of the glories which are His by virtue of the fact that He is the Creator! How wonderful are the works of God; in wisdom He hath made them all. The earth is a marvellously beautiful place after all. We know little of it. We are only scratching the surface of its wonders. But this which He by His wisdom has fabricated, this marvellous machine that works with such invariable precision, is but an index of the changelessness of God Himself. How full is this earth of the glory of the Lord, even now, had we but eyes to see!

But His revenue of glory will be derived from the cross. It is by pouring out His soul unto death, rather than by the creation of a million worlds – by the redemption of man He has won for Himself His greatest glory, for in that fact He has disclosed the qualities of His Being. He has shown us what He is. Within the theatre of this world's woes, of this world's sorrows and sins, He has manifested His glory.

'And he shall divide the spoil with the strong.' To the victor belongs the spoils. When David took his six hundred Gittites, and pursued after those who had destroyed the city of Ziklag, it is said, 'And David recovered all that the Amalekites had carried away ... there was nothing lacking to them, neither small nor great, neither sons nor daughters, neither spoil, nor any thing that they had taken to them: David recovered all.' And the people said, 'This is David's spoil. He won it by his own right arm.' I read that when the God-man died, 'having spoiled all principalities and powers, he made a shew of them openly, triumphing over them in it.'

I cannot tell you all its meaning, but I can tell you one or two things He did, and you can let a sanctified imagination picture the rest; for in this realm it would be impossible to exaggerate. For what did He come? To destroy him who has the power of death. HE DESTROYED THE POWER OF DEATH. Death no longer has any power, so far as He and His people are concerned. Within the realm of His economy, death is powerless. He uses death for His purposes, but death has no strength. He put His triumphant heel upon the neck of death, and with His wounded hand He extracted his sting and said, 'I will make it serve Me.' He sovereignly compels death to do His will; often he is made to do a servant's work. He delivered them 'who through fear of death were all their lifetime subject to bondage.' He took away the fear of death. It is not death to die, for the believer.

I cannot describe all the spoils of war. I do not know all that Jesus won back. I know that by virtue of His death for us He possessed and released a power that can entirely undo everything that sin has ever done, and restore creation to its former glory, to its Divinely-planned state when God made the world in the beginning. This poor earth has been badly beaten. It is shaking just now. I do not know what is coming within the next few months. But I do know that when the dictators have had their say, and when all the anger of men has spent itself, God in His own way, and in His own time, will speak. When the white horse and its Rider shall come down the sky, our glorious Christ will take this earth as a spoil; for 'the whole creation groaneth and travaileth in pain together until now. And not only they, but ourselves also, which have the firstfruits of the Spirit, even we ourselves groan within ourselves, waiting for the redemption of our body.' The redemption of our bodies will synchronise with the coming of the Lord Jesus Christ. His coming will be the completion of the world's redemption, and the whole creation shall be delivered into the glorious liberty of the children of God. It will be our David's spoil, for He will 'divide the spoil with the strong.'

He has given us the earnest of our inheritance here, until the redemption of the purchased possession. And that earnest has been so good, that if we had nothing more, we should have reason to praise God forever. But it is only the earnest, enough to go on with until by and by when He shall divide the spoil with the strong, we who have been weak shall be strong again, transformed into His likeness, with bodies fashioned like unto His glorious body. We shall be among the mighty men whom our David shall have. What joy unspeakable shall be ours when He 'shall divide the spoil with the strong'!

Have you received Him? Have you profited by the agony of His soul? Have you put your trust in the Saviour of sinners? If not, I beseech you to do so now. With all your heart, your intellect and will, trust Him, the Conqueror of all conquerors, the Greatest of all the great, the King of all kings! Say to Him now,

'Jesus, Thy blood and righteousness
My beauty are, my glorious dress;
'Midst flaming worlds in these arrayed,
With joy shall I lift up my head.'